MARRIAGE
On the Spiritual Path

Based on the teachings of Yogi Bhajan, PhD
Master of Kundalini Yoga

MASTERING THE HIGHEST YOGA

SHAKTI PARWHA KAUR KHALSA

MARRIAGE ON THE SPIRITUAL PATH

by Shakti Parwha Kaur Khalsa

ISBN 0-9786989-6-7

ISBN 978-0-9786989-6-6

PUBLISHED BY

Kundalini Research Institute (KRI)

P.O. Box 1819, Santa Cruz, New Mexico 87567

LAYOUT & DESIGN

Guru Raj Kaur Khalsa

COVER DESIGN

Sopurkh Singh Khalsa, GRD Design

ILLUSTRATIONS

Shabad Kaur Khalsa

This publication has received the KRI Seal of Approval. This Seal is given only to products that have been reviewed for accuracy and integrity of the sections containing the 3HO lifestyle and Kundalini Yoga as taught by Yogi Bhajan®.

DEDICATION

DEDICATED TO THE MEMORY OF
THE SIRI SINGH SAHIB
BHAI SAHIB HARBHAJAN SINGH KHALSA YOGIJI
(YOGI BHAJAN)
1929-2004

HE SAW THE GOD IN ALL

FOREWORD

Steps on the Path to a Marriage translucent to the soul and brilliant with spirit.

I ALWAYS LISTENED TO THE HEARTFELT, HOMEY AND STRAIGHT ADVICE that Shakti Parwha gave to me. She was there at my marriage—35 years ago. I am still married. And I still listen. I like her tidbits of wisdom garnered from her careful attention to her life, from our teacher Yogi Bhajan and from her experience as a wife, mother and teacher. I got the "Don't Get Married!" talk she would give to everyone, as a cautionary tale, and proceeded with all due caution and commitment. That talk has probably evolved over the years but it always retained it's solid practicality and nuanced subtleties on how to deal with commitment, polarities and the wondrous aggregation of contradictions we call the human personality.

The chapters of this book reveal Shakti and perhaps some of her secrets as a relationship chef. Her book is a tasty dish peppered with aphorisms and practical advice, leavened with humor and a twinkle in the eye and baked with the perspectives of several professionals who are yogis and healers.

The other secret about Shakti you cannot get from a book: she is a real teacher. She does not just instruct or offer advice; she puts her hand at your back and supports you in the fulfillment of your life in a thousand little ways that matter. As you read this book I suspect you will feel that same gentle hand encouraging you in your relationship, awareness and enjoyment of life.

Relationships are essential, difficult, practical and mysterious. They break us out of our carefully constructed shell, whose center is our self-concern, and expand our universe. They are mirrors in which we can perceive our self. They are worlds through which we express, feel and create.

Relationships are also circumstantial. Our ability and willingness to enter into a relationship and to sustain and nurture it to a harvest-filled maturity depends on our values, religion, family history, nature and economics. It is not just two people finding rapport, attraction and love.

Why does it seem increasingly difficult to succeed in marriage? Yogi Bhajan predicted that relationships will be extremely testing as we enter the new millennium and the Aquarian Age. One reason is that we do not accurately perceive our own nature or the effects of what we do. In fact as humans we are notoriously inept at knowing our self and predicting things that are not in the present.

A second reason is that we do not control the constant flow of thoughts from our mind. We think about our selves, think about thinking, and think about what will or will not be. It is difficult for us to be in the present and truly connect with one another as we are, beyond fears and expectations. We should think intelligently, intentionally and intuitively and not let the chatter of our mind and impulses cloud our connection to each other.

A third reason is that the circumstances have changed and will change even more. Globalization means we have many models of what a relationship should and could be. In western society we no longer have common rituals of passage that guide us into maturity and into what to do in a marriage. We are so interconnected now that we are bombarded with constant information, stimulation, commercial needs and mixed priorities; we have gained opportunity but at the cost of overwhelming noise that can sometimes distort the simple messages of trust, love and commitment that we need to give and receive in a good marriage.

A final reason for our challenge is that we are all becoming more sensitive. The increased sensitivity comes from the change of our Age to the Aquarian Time, or the social evolution of our cultures or the end of a spiritual adolescence of humanity. Whatever the reasons, we are more sensitive to each other, more defensive and more intuitive. We do not accept the masks and the games, nor the formal rights and authorities that we used to. When we connect with each other now we need the proof of the heart, experience and our perception. The institution of marriage is in its first inchoate steps of changing from a finite play of emotions, needs, and power to an Infinite game of presence, union and awareness.

As thorny as marriage may become, it is also a chance for us to experience merger with something larger than our self, to master our gender polarities in an intimate yoga, and to master the art of living less egotistically.

Shakti's book can help resolve some of the conundrums that always beset us as marriage progresses. Yogi Bhajan often repeated the quotation that "Familiarity breeds contempt." The more familiar we become, the more we reject the other. Psychology research confirms this odd phenomenon. In essence, our negative mind finds increasing numbers of mismatches as we get to know someone. Before we get to know them well, we either assume more similarity than there is or we do not confront those differences we notice. How do we become closer and more familiar and still sustain respect and love? Perhaps if we see God in our partner then there is always a part of them that is Infinite and unknown? We stay intimate by recognizing the Infinite.

We want to be truthful and disclose our self to our partner. But candor that reveals everything is often harmful. How do we discharge our true self directly, being real, so we can have understanding and dialogue? Yogi Bhajan said to use a technique called "harmonious communication" that starts by accepting the other completely. Then learn the language of each other. Men and women communicate differently. The masculine and the feminine have their own modes. Words are heard and processed differently. Recently I saw a brain study that showed that though women's brains are physically slightly smaller on the average than men's, women's brains have more dense neurons with better connections especially in the area of language and understanding. Words are experienced and processed differently. How do we speak to be heard, listen to really hear, and learn to read between the lines to know what our partner really needs?

To have a great marriage, a deep spiritual and powerfully pragmatic relationship, there are attitudes, skills, techniques and the wisdom of experience that can smooth our way. As you read this book and you cull out the special ideas and inspirations that speak to you, I hope you will be fortified and uplifted to enjoy the gift of relationship. I can only say, from my personal and professional (as counselor and yogi) experience, that it is possible for each of us to have a wonderful marriage that deepens through time, stays fresh as if new, and brings constant challenges to keep you awake and aware.

Gurucharan Singh Khalsa PhD, LPCC
Director of Training, Kundalini Research Institute

ACKNOWLEDGEMENTS

IN HOLLYWOOD, CALIFORNIA, it's Awards time. In December, big ads are splashed across the pages of the LA Times: *For Your Consideration*. The Motion Picture Academy of Arts and Science is going to give out shiny "Oscars." The Foreign Press will hand out Golden Globes for outstanding contributions made by those involved in the many aspects of filmmaking. There are "Emmys" for TV winners, "Grammys" for Country Music Singers, and "Tonys" for Stage productions. If I could give an award to the many people who shared their time and their talents to create this book, I think it would be a gold "Yogi" —with platinum and diamonds! But in lieu of the statuette (in prayer pose perhaps?), I want to express my heartfelt thanks (in no particular order) to:

Siri Ram Kaur, whose engagement was the catalyst for getting this book in motion, and Harijot Kaur who helped create its title.

Ellisa Kerluhas who helped organize and edit the early draft. Nam Kaur and Satya Kaur of KRI who read it and asked questions that needed to be asked (and answered).

Satgur Prasad Singh (age 22), my personal computer consultant. His mother, Ek Ong Kar Kaur Khalsa, whose meticulous editing and proofreading is unparalleled.

My four Ph.D. friends—the Psychologists who, out of the kindness of their hearts, took time to write their insightful "Professionally Speaking" articles—just because I asked them to: Dr. Sat-Kaur Khalsa; Dr. Shanti Shanti Kaur Khalsa, Dharam Dev Kaur Khalsa, and Dr. Guru Terath Kaur Khalsa.

Then there's dear Deva Kaur Khalsa of Florida, who encouraged her students to write their experiences for this book.

Special thanks to each of the writers who courageously bared their souls and their lives to share their inspiring "Up Close and Personal" stories: Siri Ved Kaur Khalsa; Guru Meher Kaur Khalsa; Ra-el Corsini aka Sarb Nam Kaur; Sat Jivan Kaur Khalsa;

Elsa Fox; Hari Bhajan Kaur Khalsa; Siri Pritham Kaur Khalsa; Guru Mustuk Singh Khalsa; Siri Atma Kaur Khalsa; Dr. Siri Atma Singh Khalsa (no, they are not related); and extra appreciation for Guruka Singh Khalsa who also expertly edited Yogi Bhajan's lecture on sex.

I am so pleased that Shabad Kaur Khalsa, who illustrated my first book, agreed to do the drawings for this one, translating some of the concepts into images, pictures that, as has been said, "are worth a thousand words."

I can't thank Guru Raj Kaur Khalsa enough, not only for her excellence in interior page layout and design, but also for her valuable editorial suggestions and excellent photo finds.

I must express appreciation for SoPurkh Singh Khalsa's keeping up until his beautiful cover art design was completed to my satisfaction.

And finally, he who is last shall be first: I thank God for bringing me my Teacher, Siri Singh Sahib, Bhai Sahib Harbhajan Singh Khalsa Yogiji (Yogi Bhajan).

(Note: With all the help I received—and it was amazing—I take total personal responsibility for any errors or flaws in this book.)

PREFACE

Why am I writing a book about marriage? Well, mainly because, Yogi Bhajan told me to! It just took me a while to actually do it. I definitely had plenty of material, because for over 35 years I had the privilege of learning from him, the most extraordinary Teacher, Master of Kundalini Yoga, and superb master of the art of living. I spent hours and hours listening to him. He was training people how to make the most of being alive, how to be truly human. He taught that everyone has a right to be successful and happy—in life and in love. I took notes.

Statistics show relationships and marriages these days are one disaster after another. People are suffering and miserable, disappointed and often betrayed. Marriage, divorce, marriage, divorce—like being caught in a revolving door, people are going around in self-defeating circles. It doesn't have to be that way. The principles that Yogi Bhajan taught can empower us to change the pattern. We can transform ourselves and as we change, the people around us change.

Yogi Bhajan not only revealed ancient yogic techniques, but also gave practical day-to-day (and night-to-night) advice—that really works.

Before John Gray's popular book, *Men are From Mars, Women are From Venus*, was published, Yogi Bhajan explained in great detail the fundamental differences between the sexes. He gave practical suggestions, and taught methods that enable men and women to co-exist in harmony, and be truly happy and fulfilled in relationships. Ignorance is not bliss, whereas knowing who you really are, and understanding the unique nature of your partner, gives you a tremendous advantage in making a success of your marriage.

This book is based on Yogi Bhajan's teachings, plus the experience I have had counseling as a Sikh Dharma minister, and the "Mother of 3HO," a role I was assigned by Yogi Bhajan in 1969, when he established the Healthy, Happy, Holy Organization.

HOW THIS BOOK WAS BORN

In 1986 Yogi Bhajan told me to write a book about Kundalini Yoga. It took me quite a while to get to it. Finally, in 1996, *KUNDALINI YOGA: The Flow of Eternal Power* was published. Someone asked him, "Sir, what should Shakti write now?" He said, "She should write a book on marriage." I thought, "Oh, No!" But like a good student, I kept silent. I filed his suggestion in the back of my mind (way back) and conveniently forgot about it, until May of 2005.

That spring, my friend and colleague, Siri Ram Kaur Khalsa, announced her engagement to Jai Singh Khalsa. I joked with her and said, "If you're planning to get married, I'd better give you my famous 'Don't Get Married' talk." Then it hit me; I remembered what Yogi Bhajan had said in 1986, and I realized it was time to write this book.

Besides gathering my personal notes from Yogi Bhajan's lectures, I enlisted the aid of my 3HO and Sikh Dharma family and friends, recognized experts in their fields with the requisite initials after their names, and asked them to share their thoughts and experiences as marriage counselors. They have written some excellent articles you can find in the "Professionally Speaking" section.

I can tell you that using the teachings of Yogi Bhajan has revolutionized thousands of lives, preserved the sacredness, and brought happiness back into countless marriages. However, as he used to say, "Doing is Believing." So, it is my hope that you will read these pages with an open mind and then try "doing," so you can experience the results for yourself. Here are the guidelines; may all who enter here be blessed!

Shakti Parwha Kaur Khalsa,
Los Angeles, December 2006

CONTENTS

INTRODUCTION

"Marriage is the highest yoga. The Shiva-Shakti[1]
union on earth is the counterpart of Divine Union."
Yogi Bhajan

Most of us don't think of ourselves as spiritual beings, but we are. We are actually and truly immortal souls, divine beings temporarily traveling through time and space in human bodies. According to ancient philosophy it is a fact that each of us is on a spiritual journey of Self-rediscovery, whether we know it or not. Those who have experienced this truth tell us the journey eventually leads back to the divine source of all life, our true Home. They have offered us road maps to follow so we can reach the same destination.

"One thing to remember is: All things come from God and all things shall return to God."[2]

Marriage is the kind of "yoga" in which two people walking a spiritual path together, help and support each other around the potholes and over the rough patches and unexpected detours. Marriage is one of the best, though certainly not the easiest, roads to take on this journey. It provides an opportunity to achieve one of the greatest fulfillments in life: divine union with a partner.

The word "yoga" means to join, yoke, or unite. Unite what? Your individual consciousness with the Universal consciousness. This merger, the expansion beyond the limitations of the little self, is the ultimate goal of all yogas. This Divine Union is the purpose of life—and Marriage.

Knowing this ideal you can use it as a touchstone to measure your intentions, aspirations, and actions. At the same time, practical wisdom suggests that before you tie the knot, take the plunge, walk down the aisle, you consider the down-to-earth realities, and look at the day-to-day challenges you are bound to face in any marriage.

IN THIS BOOK I'M GOING TO GIVE YOU A RECIPE FOR A SUCCESSFUL MARRIAGE, and list the main ingredients you need to make it work. I'll also point out the things that can turn the sweetest blend bitter. Most of the advice is just plain common sense. But in addition we have the benefit of the enlightened guidance of Yogi Bhajan Ph.D., Master of Kundalini Yoga, who knew exactly how to poke, provoke, confront and then elevate the consciousness of everyone he met. His teachings, and his very being, touched and transformed the lives of thousands of people throughout the world.

Included on these pages are transcripts of some of Yogi Bhajan's insightful, and often blunt, comments on marriage as well as his suggestions for specific meditations and mantras that can transform a marriage. I asked some people who have tried them to share their experiences. I think you will find their testimonials fascinating; I know I did. In addition, there is a translation of the sacred wedding vows written by the great Master of Raj Yoga, Guru Ram Das, fourth Sikh Guru, for his own wedding.

I realize that looking at marriage primarily as a shared spiritual path is a far cry from the present day, almost casual, attitude toward marriage that is especially prevalent in the West. However, I believe that no matter what your religion or belief system may be, you will find these concepts and practices useful as tools to enhance your relationships. Life was meant for joy! May you create a truly happy and harmonious home filled with love.

By presenting a more sacred model for marriage, based on the universal teachings of Yogi Bhajan, which include the sacred science of Kundalini Yoga, the 3HO way of life, Humanology, and the technology found in Sikh Dharma, I hope to prevent disappointment, dispel unrealistic expectations, and, God willing, lower the divorce rate.

3HO and Kundalini Yoga have a symbiotic relationship with Sikh Dharma and I am grateful to share technology from all of these sources. However, you don't have to be a Sikh or even practice Kundalini Yoga to benefit from the ideas on these pages.

Are you planning to get married? I hope so. Whether it's tomorrow, next week, ten years from now (or even if it was last year), I humbly submit the information in this book with the hope and prayer that you may find it useful before and during your marriage.

May God and Guru bless you and your spouse to live in your excellence as "two bodies with one soul."

*"The institution of marriage is a union of two polarities
to go through everything devotedly. Where there
is emotional upset, what devotion is there?"*

Yogi Bhajan July 8, 1978

HOW IT ALL BEGAN
ALONG CAME THE YOGI

ARRANGED MARRIAGES? GOOD GRIEF!
Picture this. It's June of 1969. "The Yogi" has been teaching in Los Angeles since January, and now he's been invited by a group of his students: spiritual seekers, baby boomers known as "flower children" and disdained by the Establishment as "hippies" (actually this particular group called themselves "The Juke Savages"), to attend a Summer Solstice celebration in New Mexico.

This rebellious generation (born in the late '40's and '50's) rejected the restraints of anything organized, formal, or limiting. They were a generation of free spirits—born to manifest the Aquarian Consciousness that was just dawning. They were bursting to break out of conventional buttoned up society. It was a wild time. "Free love" was rampant. Yogi Bhajan saw beneath their undisciplined actions and as he looked into their souls; he saw their potential for excellence. He opened his heart to them, embraced their longing to experience God, and gave them his unconditional love. He set about training students to become teachers, giving them a path to follow, technology that could heal their bodies, clear their minds and purify their emotions, and allow them to fulfill their destinies.

He told them, "It is your birthright to be Healthy, Happy, and Holy and Kundalini Yoga is the tool to use." Young people came by the droves to sit at his feet, learn and practice. Most of the students thronging to Yogi Bhajan's Kundalini Yoga classes were in their mid to late teens or early twenties. They caravanned in psychedelic Volkswagen busses to Los Angeles and at that first Summer Solstice yoga camp in New Mexico many couples decided to marry because Yogiji enthusiastically championed the spiritual value of the marriage commitment. He pointed out, "There is no freedom that is free." He also taught, "There's no liberation without labor."

With the insight of a yoga master, he could see when, how, and if a couple could progress spiritually as marriage partners. He knew from a karmic standpoint if they belonged together. Asking his blessing, they decided to marry, and he performed many marriages on the spot at Summer Solstices.

But after the honeymoon (and sometimes during it!), in the cold gray light of dawn, couples who had been totally enthralled with each other while they were meditating together during the heightened awareness of the Solstice energy, found they were no longer in that blissful, elevated, soul-to-soul consciousness. Now they were faced with the practical routine and demands of day-to-day living. Having to get along with someone who was virtually a stranger was not easy. They didn't know what to expect and what not to expect from each other. They were unhappy. Anger and resentment surfaced.

SHAKTI'S FAMOUS "DON'T GET MARRIED" TALK

I was concerned that they would blame Yogi Bhajan for "making" them get married. So before more weddings took place, I started counseling couples, giving what came to be known as Shakti's "Don't Get Married" talk. I explained that just because Yogiji

had agreed to, or even suggested their engagement, did not mean that they had to get married, it only meant that he saw their potential to fulfill their individual destiny by working out their karma together as a couple. It was up to them to figure out the details.

I tried to give them a reality check before they plunged into marriage. I didn't want them to have false expectations. I pointed out that a successful marriage doesn't just happen; it takes applied intelligence, understanding, flexibility, and continuous conscious effort.

Two souls may be perfectly attuned, but what about when their egos clash? (And they usually will.) What about the petty annoyances and strange personal habits of another person? What if one is compulsively neat and organized, and the other creates clutter all over the place? The "Odd Couple," Felix and Oscar, made for great television comedy, but in a marriage, the combination is no laughing matter.

Nothing is trivial. Seemingly little things can pile up and build an insurmountable wall of frustration and resentment. Most important, what about understanding, accepting, and adjusting to the fundamental differences in the emotional and psychological make-up of the opposite sex?

To make a success of marriage, to truly enjoy it as a "carriage unto Infinity," husband and wife really need to share the same fundamental aspirations and ideals. They need to respect each other's ideas. Their job is to supplement and complement each other. (Offering genuine compliments now and then doesn't hurt, either.)

Egos and past experiences can easily get in the way of the deep and abiding love and trust that should develop between husband and wife. Too often the past pollutes the present and destroys the future.

Traveling through life together holding on to shared ideals without getting bogged down by the stress and complications of daily living is a big challenge. Yet it can be done when you have a clear map that shows the best route to your shared destination: a loving marriage that upholds each individual while honoring the sanctity of the divine union—and doesn't lose sight of the ultimate goal of life. This book is an expanded version of my famous "Don't Get Married" talk.

CHAPTER TWO

LEARNING TO BE HUMAN
IN FOUR STAGES

I t has been said that we are born divine and we are here on Earth to learn how to be human.

Mostly what we have to learn as human beings, we learn from relationships. Lessons start even before Kindergarten, and when we get there we are taught to share, to play nicely with others, and "follow the rules" (no hitting, don't take Johnny's toy without asking, hang up your coat, put your crayons away neatly). Lessons change and get a lot more complicated as we mature.

The ancients taught that we learn how to live as human beings in four stages. Each stage of life is intended to teach specific skills toward the path of enlightenment. In this book, we are concerned with the second stage, the period in life of what they called the "Householder," during which couples marry. But first here's an overview of all four stages so you can see how the course of human life was defined.

STAGE ONE. The first 25 years of life was called *Brahmacharya*. It was a time of celibacy, a time to grow up and mature, to study and prepare to take on the responsibilities of an adult. Time to focus on personal growth—mentally, emotionally, and spiritually.

STAGE TWO. From 25 to 50 was for married life, to experience all its joys and challenges. This second classroom in the school of life was called *Ghrist Ashram*. In mar-

riage, the life of a householder, men and women devote themselves to the care of a spouse and a family. Instead of focusing only on oneself, one learns to put others first. Marriage provides the opportunity for a person to become less selfish and self absorbed. This is a big step forward in consciousness.

> *Ghrist Ashram, mahan ashram, devee dev poojde.*
> "This household life is so great that the angels and divine worship it."3

The first great Sikh Saint and Master, Guru Nanak, who himself was married, taught that rather than being an obstacle to spiritual development, as many ascetics and renunciates believed, marriage was "the highest yoga."4 The Guru recommended marriage to his followers, who were known as *shishyas* (students of truth: Sikhs), and said that married life was ideal for them.

STAGE THREE. After age 50, it was assumed you had gained enough spiritual insight, practical knowledge and wisdom to teach, and so it was time to travel with your spouse and share what you had learned. You became a teacher. As a teacher, you expand your service, reaching out to guide the greater human family.

People learn in two ways, either in the hands of Time (which is usually pretty painful), or in the hands of a Teacher (which can make the path, if not smoother, at least easier to navigate).

STAGE FOUR. Traditionally, from age 75 to 100 the soul longs only to be with God, and that is when people retired to their little **kutya** (hut) in the forest or the mountains, devoting themselves to prayer and meditation. Devotees came to sit at the feet of these wise elders who emerged periodically to bless and instruct.

Those of us now living in the 21st Century don't have to take these time lines as etched in stone, but it's useful to look at them from the standpoint of what each stage offers. Even if you get married when you are younger than 25, or don't get married until you're in your fifties or sixties, no matter how old you are, the same principles and lessons of *Ghrist Ashram* apply. The task is to unite together, living as one soul in two bodies.

Marriage is an important factor in the fulfillment of your personal destiny. Life as a householder can be a challenge or an opportunity, bringing happiness or misery, depending upon how you relate to your spouse, and how strongly you relate to the soul in yourself and each other. Developing self-awareness and your own connection to the Infinite will help carry you through the ups and downs that every marriage experiences.

*"The greatest education man has to learn is not medical science, not sociology,
not chemistry, not biology, not mathematics, but the science of man, the science of self.
The science of self and self-awareness is the highest knowledge a man can possess
because then you can pull through all circumstances."*
Yogi Bhajan, The Teachings of Yogi Bhajan

CHAPTER THREE

UNION

*"God becomes the servant of those who amalgamate
their egos and bring one identity out of the union
of the two. They are such that God grants them the
soul through which their generations will live forever.
That is how saints are born on the earth."*

Yogi Bhajan

AMALGAMATION: BUILDING THE INSTITUTION OF MARRIAGE

As husband and wife, you are literally building something new together; you are creating a whole new entity. That's why they call it the institution of marriage. It takes constant, conscious effort to build this institution. It won't spring up overnight in its final form. Patience and steady efforts are required.

Patience pays; otherwise even stones are heavy for a man.

Yogi Bhajan

Each marriage has a life of its own, its own identity, its own qualities. Marriage is greater than, and actually different from, the sum of its individual parts. It is an amalgam, a merger, a partnership in which, to be successful, each partner has to invest 100% of his or her self. No reservations. The idea that marriage is a 50/50 partnership just isn't good enough. Yogiji used to say that 50/50 makes marriage into a business deal! And that's not what it's supposed to be.

HAPPILY EVER AFTER...NOT!

For some of us (mostly girls), the fantasy about romance and marriage begins in childhood with fairy tales: With just a kiss, frogs become handsome princes, Sleeping Beauty wakes up, and then, of course, there is Cinderella. Maybe that's where the idea of living "happily ever after" (apparently effortlessly) began. That fiction has been glamorized through love songs, romance novels, and old-time movies. Despite the huge number of divorces today many people still cling to the illusion that getting married is a *guarantee* of happiness. It isn't. But it can be a dynamic *means* toward happiness if it is understood as a spiritual endeavor. Remember, marriage is "the highest yoga," so it takes practice to perfect it. Let's look at some common myths about love and relationships.

WHAT IS LOVE?

Love is a tough thing to define. Poets have tried. Songwriters have tried. But usually what they're writing about is romance, attachment, dependency, desire, and, yes, lust, but that's not love.

> *"A man loves a woman because she inspires him, takes him out*
> *of the mundane to experience his infinite self."* [5]

Real love is different from "falling in love," which is a temporary state of mild (or severe) insanity, a condition of euphoria, in which you are totally engulfed by your emotions and wrapped up in the object of your affections. He or she seems perfect. You can't think about anything else, you don't *want* to think about anything else. This rosy state of romantic fantasy makes you feel like you're walking on air. The birds are singing, the sun is shining on a perfect world that consists of just you and the object of your affection. This delightful condition is a temporary gift, no doubt designed by the Creator to encourage propagation of the species. Sometimes it's called infatuation. It is temporary. It is unrealistic to expect it to last. I'm sorry to say, it inevitably wears off. Hopefully it is replaced with the enduring power of actual love, which is a heart-centered reality, characterized by a constant desire to give, and comprised of kindness, compassion, and self-sacrifice. Sacrifice means to make sacred— and that is what actually brings Happiness.

True love is unconditional love. It is conscious, compassionate, and caring. And, unlike what is sometimes mistakenly labeled love, true love is not a business deal, it doesn't depend upon what you get, rather it is based on what you give of yourself. Not "things." "I'll love you if...." If you give me gifts, send me roses and take me to fancy restaurants, etc. is not love. Not that there's anything wrong with gifts, roses, and fancy restaurants if you can afford them, but love can't be measured in material terms. True love grows deeper and stronger with time; it doesn't wear off or wear out.

I found this poen by Yogi Bhajan about love in my files:

> Love gives you the power to merge,
> From finite to Infinity.
> Love gives you the power to trust,
> From nothing to everything.
>
> Love gives you power, the powerful prayer
> Between you and your Creator.
> Love gives you vastness,
> As vast as there can be.
>
> Love gives you the hold, the experience,
> And the touch with your own infinity,
> As beautiful, bountiful and blissful
> As there can be.

Here's another way he defined it: *"Love is the ultimate state of human behavior where compassion prevails and kindness rules."* Yogi Bhajan truly loved everyone, and he lived it.

VIVA LA DIFFERENCE! MAC'S AND PC'S

We humans are manufactured in two distinct makes and models. All men may be created equal, but men and women were created different. Obviously men have different hardware, but it's the unique software that really makes the difference in how men and women function. We are wired differently. Men and women are fundamentally different. That can't be repeated too often. As Yogi Bhajan said:

"Women are exactly the opposite from men—they have nothing in common. It is only the mysterious thing called love which brings them together. We cannot know what is going on inside the other's head. Admit that you do not know what the other's world is like. Just agree that you each have the right to be who you are." [6]

It is unrealistic to expect your spouse to feel, think, plan, or respond in any given situation as you would, or the way your (same gender) best friend might. False expectations lead to disappointment, disappointment leads to frustration, and frustration leads to anger—not a happy sequence, so it's best to know at the outset what to expect and what not to expect from your partner.

GRACE AND DIGNITY

It is the responsibility of the man to maintain his wife's grace, and it is the responsibility of the woman to maintain her husband's dignity—and this means not only in public, but also in their communications behind closed doors. Harsh, rude words once spoken will never be forgotten. Women, keep in mind that despite any macho appearance, a man's ego is fragile, and if you say something to hurt him, he will never forget it. He may not show it, but he will resent you for it. If you continue, sooner or later, he's liable to leave you.

SUN AND MOON

These two cosmic symbols provide an excellent analogy for understanding the inherent nature of the male and the female. Man is like the sun and the woman is like the moon. Earth depends on both of them. The sun is steady and shines forth, the moon waxes and wanes and reflects the light of the sun. Does that mean that man should always be center stage? Does it mean a woman has no light of her own? No. Analogies can only go so far. So, it doesn't mean that a woman cannot, or should

not be successful personally and professionally as well as in her role as wife and mother. Especially in today's economy where two incomes are often needed, a wife often has to work. But if she wants to make her husband happy (and thus ensure her own happiness), she reflects his light back to him, and makes him feel like a king in his home. A man has to feel that

he is the provider (even if she makes more money than he does), and both partners need to feel valued and respected by each other.

It doesn't take a lot. Little things, little sweet kindnesses, little words of love, gestures expressing genuine appreciation set a loving, harmonious vibration. Remember the *One Minute Manager* by Kenneth Blanchard and Spencer Johnson? The concept of successful management was to offer a pat on the back, or a word of appreciation immediately on the spot when you noticed a positive performance by an employee. It's rather obvious that encouragement and recognition motivate positive behavior. So, applying that principle to your relationship, when you "catch" your spouse doing something nice, speak up right away, You can say something like, "Thank you, darling, I really appreciate that." Or even just, "God bless you, thank you." It just requires paying attention to what he or she is doing for you, instead of taking everything for granted. Writing little love notes and putting them in his lunch box, or under her pillow, make day-to-day living fun and can keep that spark of mutual admiration glowing. Thoughtful loving gestures, big or small, can help cement the loving bond growing between you.

To successfully amalgamate and create a successful (and that includes "happy") marriage requires conscious, consistent effort; in other words, you have to work at it all the time! It's like when you're driving a car, especially uphill, you have to keep your foot on the gas pedal all the time, or you're going to lose ground, go sliding down and most likely have an accident.

Enough of that analogy, let's get on to our next topic: the three main ingredients in the Recipe for Happiness.

RECIPE FOR HAPPINESS

*"Love is a self-sacrifice. Love is the experience within one's self of
one's own selflessness; that's why love is God. No one can explain
love, because love is ecstasy. Love is the essence of an ever-longing
devotion. Love does not change. If love changes, it is not love."*

The Teachings of Yogi Bhajan

There are three main ingredients needed to build and maintain a happy and
mutually fulfilling marriage:

▸ Commitment
▸ Trust
▸ Communication

COMMITMENT

The commitment you make when you get married is a promise to God and to each
other that you intend to stay married, come what may. "In sickness or in health, for
richer or poorer"—no matter how old you get, or how circumstances change.
Marriage is a sacred, lifetime commitment. It isn't just a license to have sex for a while
until the excitement wears off. If you think for even one moment, "Well, if it does-
n't work out, we can always get a divorce," then you don't understand the meaning
of commitment nor the meaning of marriage.

Commitment means to Keep Up! as Yogi Bhajan often roared during yoga class.
It means you're not going to quit, no matter how tired you are or how sore your
"relating" muscles are. The Dictionary defines commitment as a pledge, a promise to
fulfill an obligation of trust. Fulfilling that commitment, honoring your vows means
you are a person of integrity.

A few years ago during a panel discussion about marriage, one of the married members said, "Marriage is like being on a roller coaster; you don't jump out of your seat because the ride is plunging down a steep scary slope." You may scream, but you hang on for dear life—clinging to each other.

In a true marriage, the mutual commitment to keeping up and maintaining the shared aspiration to grow together on the same spiritual path toward the same goal becomes the touchstone you use whenever the road gets bumpy. And the road undoubtedly will get bumpy. When it does, that's the time to remember the divine purpose of marriage:

> "Marriage is an exalted state of consciousness where
> two people practice to become One Divine Being." [7]

Realistically, maintaining your attitude toward your marriage in those exalted terms 24/7 is not easy. When problems arise, couples need ways to remind themselves and each other to see the bigger picture. That's why meditation and consistent spiritual practice[8] are so important.

There may be times when you don't feel "happy." But those are the times when it's more important than ever to keep up. The true nature of the soul is joy, so when we're not happy, it's because we're out of touch with the divine part of ourselves. Happiness has to do with connecting with our core identity. Your yoga and meditation practices are the tools to help you attain this state of union within yourself. Then from that connection you can share your joy and love with your partner with an attitude of gratitude. Gratitude multiplies happiness.

The value of a mutual commitment can't be emphasized too strongly. Commitment is the crucial first step on what Yogi Bhajan set as the "Seven Steps to Happiness." He often said, "Keep up and you'll be kept up." Making the effort brings the blessing of support from your higher Self.

If you want to make a success of your marriage, you will want to recognize and climb these Seven Steps to Happiness:

Seven Steps to Happiness [9]

1st Step—Commitment
to kindness and compassion; it gives you Character.

2nd Step—Character
is a pattern of behavior where you can clearly answer
and stand before your own consciousness. It leads to Dignity.

3rd Step—Dignity
is when you act as a god for another; then you gain Divinity.

4th Step—Divinity
is when you put yourself and your life on the line to serve another person
or a creature, which leads you to Grace.

5th Step—Grace
is when you've developed a presence that works
so that you have the Power to Sacrifice.

6th Step—Power to Sacrifice
is when God sits in your heart and presides in your head
and you can therefore sacrifice—and that takes you to Happiness.

7th Step—Happiness
is when you can give thanks for being these seven things.

Yogi Bhajan KWTC 1989

TRUST

Perhaps Trust precedes Commitment, but they go hand in hand. Whichever way you view these ingredients, we can safely say that trust, often rare and fragile in today's world, is essential to a happy marriage. You have to trust that your spouse is going to be faithful to you.

You trust each other despite past betrayals and disappointments by others. It's not fair, and definitely counterproductive, to distrust your husband or wife because someone in your past was unfaithful to you. Despite any previous unhappy relationship, you don't bring that negative expectation into the present relationship. This is especially important if you've been married before. Don't automatically assign your previous spouse's virtues or vices to your current partner. Let the past go. Yogi Bhajan emphasized, "Those who live in the past have no future."

The commitment that builds trust, if you are a woman is: from this moment onward, you promise to relate to every other man as your father, brother, or son. For a man, you commit to viewing every other woman as a mother, sister, or daughter. You don't flirt. Period.

Trust eliminates the possibility of jealousy, the green-eyed monster that undermines and damages many relationships. When you trust each other, you know that you can depend on each other; there's no insecurity or worry about whether he/she might be attracted to someone else, have an affair, or leave you.

Childhood memories can also undermine a marriage. For instance, suppose you had a difficult and even painful relationship with your father who was an abusive alcoholic. Let's say Dad had the habit of scratching his left ear. Then suppose one morning, sitting innocently at the breakfast table, your husband happens to scratch his left ear. Well, like Pavlov's dog, your subconscious can trigger a conditioned response of fear and anger. You may start shouting at him. The poor guy won't have any idea what he's done wrong. You yourself may not understand why you're upset.

At that moment, it's important to remember that trusting your spouse is a spiritual practice within itself. By trusting your partner, the known, you develop the capacity to trust God, the Unknown.

"Remember one law which I have learned: Those who do not learn to belong to a man whom they love, will never know the art of belonging to a God whom they will never know."

Yogi Bhajan, The Teachings of Yogi Bhajan

Trust becomes even stronger when you include the third essential ingredient of this special recipe for happiness:

COMMUNICATION

How well do you really know the person who is going to be sharing your time and your space? What you don't know can hurt you!

It is only common sense to find out as much as you can about each other before you even consider promising to spend the rest of your lives together. That takes being able to communicate comfortably and effectively on topics that will affect your marriage.

The first and foremost discussion you need to have is about spiritual values. Marriage is intended to create a sacred bond; so sharing the same religious faith is a major consideration. Interfaith marriages put a huge strain on a marriage, complicating an already challenging relationship. In the fog of romantic illusion before marriage the question of religion is sometimes ignored, and after you marry, it can be buried and stifled in a maze of mundane details for quite a while.

Have you considered these questions? [10]
- Do you share the same philosophy of life? Same religious beliefs?
- Are you both on the same page when it comes to the major decisions you're going to face?
- What are your goals in life?
- Do you share some of each other's major aspirations?
- What are your core values?
- Should the wife have a career?
- How do you feel about having children?
- Do you have the same approach to raising children?

- Do you want to live in the city or the country?
- Do you like the same kinds of food?
  (You're going to be eating a lot of meals together.)
- How will you handle money? Do you stick to a budget or spend what you have?
- What expectations and feelings do you have about sexual relations?

An ounce of prevention is worth a pound of cure. Don't wait until after the honeymoon to talk openly and honestly with each other about what marriage means to each of you. Talk about the big things and the little things.

My psychologist friends tell me that problems over sex and money are the two major causes of divorce. An example is when one spouse wants to stay within the budget, paying bills on time, while the other thinks nothing of being extravagant and piling up debt.

As for dealing with finances, here's some practical information from the *LA Times*, Sunday, May 29, 2005:

HEADLINE: MONEY TALK

"Spouses need to consult with each other on big purchases"
One would think that such a common sense policy would be obvious, but apparently it's not. The article printed a question from a woman who wrote that her husband recently went to buy a new minivan for her (they have three little children), but instead traded their car in on a new smaller car—which they couldn't afford. They were in debt, now are in deeper debt, and she's definitely not happy. The article went on to say:

> *"Most financially savvy couples have an agreement that they'll consult each other on any purchases over a certain $ amount…depending on their circumstances."*

So, before you marry, have the "money" talk! You'll probably be sharing a bankbook as well as a bed. Better find out as much as you can how to make both of them comfortable.

I was actually surprised to read[11] that Yogi Bhajan recommended that women handle the finances and manage the budget! He said if the wife doesn't know how

Enough.

to balance the checkbook, the husband should teach her. "This shows her that you believe in her." But he also says later[12]:

"There cannot be a general law, because humans are different.... Everybody differs from everybody else, everybody's circumstances differ; everybody's aspect and prospect are different; everybody's moods, needs and faculties are different from everybody else's as are their desires, body odor, physical approach, and mental approach. We must understand in 3HO we put our greatest emphasis on respecting individuality and individual privacy. We believe that if an individual is strong, society is strong. And a strong society will provide a shelter for the individual. Therefore, our main objective is to build a strong individual.

"Now here we are in a men's course. We want to build a strong man of you. Not so that you become macho; not so you become self-destructive; but so that you can handle every challenge you face. We believe the strength of the man is in the challenge. The higher the challenge, the higher the man's capacity to meet it, the higher is his achievement in life. Challenge is not something which destroys you; challenge is something which gives you an experience...."

Getting to know as much as you can about each other's differences, attitudes (about money, for instance!) and habits—ahead of time—can avoid the kind of surprises that cause anger and resentment later on. In real estate the highest value is placed on "location, location, location." In marriage it's communication, communication, communication.

A FEW THINGS TO TALK ABOUT

Allergies	Finances	Religious convictions
Aspirations	Goals in Life	Sense of Humor—does he/she "get" you?
Careers	Health Issues	
Children	In-Laws	Sex
Community Service	Past experiences [13]	Spiritual Practice
Dietary preferences	Pets	Sports interests
Entertainment preferences	Pet peeves	Travel
Exercise habits	Political views	Where to live

SETTLING DIFFERENCES

Communication doesn't mean that you discuss every little thing, or analyze every gesture and word that is said, but if something is really bugging you, don't let it fester. You need to be able to talk honestly with each other. If you keep annoyance bottled up, it leads to frustration, and frustration can finally explode into an angry "burst out."

Picture this: It's time to sleep. Your husband flings the windows open wide to get fresh air, but you're shivering with cold. What do you do? How do you work this out so that it's a win-win situation instead of one of you feeling angry and resentful? Communication. You've got to learn how to communicate successfully so that you can settle differences without fighting. Bottling up your emotions is not the solution.

As Yogi Bhajan said:

> *"All sickness, all shallowness, all unhappiness, all pain, all miseries*
> *are the outcome of one source: keeping negativity within yourself."*
>
> The Teachings of Yogi Bhajan

You have the responsibility to let the other person know when and if there's a problem. But the way you communicate is really important.

Watch the words that you use. Avoid confronting language. Words to avoid: "You always…" or "You never…do such and such, etc."

A better way to express your problem (and the problem is *yours* if you're the one reacting) is to say something like, "I'm sure you don't know that when you do that, it makes me feel_____." That way you're not blaming the other person. You are taking responsibility for your own feelings while you're letting it be known that a certain behavior or habit is causing a problem for you. Also, watch your tone of voice. If your intent is to create mutual understanding, then kindness and respect will vibrate in your voice. If you're talking just to complain or criticize, that will be obvious, and you won't accomplish anything except to create defensiveness and possibly hostility.

Whether it's a major issue or something seemingly trivial like humming or head scratching, leaving dirty dishes in the sink or dirty socks on the floor, never blame your spouse for *your* feelings. One of you may want the house to be neat as a pin, and the other is just simply a slob by nature. This kind of situation isn't fun and requires careful communication. Moreover it probably requires you both to modify your attitudes and behaviors to find middle ground.

How flexible are you? What is your level of tolerance for ways of doing things that are different from yours? These are some of the questions to explore *before* you get married.

The world would be a much better place if all of us would consider how our words are going to be received and perceived before we let them escape our lips. Many times we are more polite and considerate of strangers than we are when talking with our own family. Watch your language. Think fast but speak slowly.

Disagreements are only natural between any two human beings, but the way to resolve them is through communication, not confrontation.

If you want a positive result from any communication, it's best to be polite. One of the children's books I used to read to my son explained it this way:

"Politeness is to do and say the kindest thing in the kindest way."

WORDS FOR WOMEN
(MEN MAY WANT TO READ THIS TO UNDERSTAND WOMEN A LITTLE BETTER!)

"First recognize the creativity of the Creator. The moment a woman recognizes and understands that she is the creativity of the Creator, confidence as a woman comes to her."

The Teachings of Yogi Bhajan

CHICKS INTO EAGLES

The French have a saying, "Viva la difference." The problem is that instead of appreciating and valuing our differences, men and women keep fighting the age-old battle of the sexes. With Women's Lib, the battle escalated and took on a different dimension. Unfortunately, in fighting for equal wages for equal work, a valid cause, many women lost sight of their unique God-given gifts of being female.

When Yogi Bhajan started teaching women how to utilize their inherent abilities and capabilities, and reclaim the respect they should be accorded, he called it "Changing Chicks into Eagles." Determined to empower women so they would never

be exploited sexually, socially, professionally or psychologically, he created a summer training camp just for women and lectured extensively on many pertinent subjects. His lectures were amazing and transformed the lives of the women fortunate enough to hear him. I strongly urge all women, especially brides-to-be, to read the transcripts of these "Women in Training" manuals,[14] so you can truly understand who you are, how to be happy, how to make your husband happy, and how to make the most of your Shakti[15] power. Yogi Bhajan taught that woman is the Grace of God, and gave a special meditation of the same name for all women to experience their divinity.[16]

TALK, TALK, TALK

You may be the exception, but most of us women talk too much.

We often want to hash over every little thing that happens. Most men are not like that. They don't like a lot of chatter and usually don't want to get into deep psychological discussions with their wives, especially about their wives' neuroses.

At Khalsa Women's Training Camp, July 25, 1992, Yogi Bhajan advised women:

"Never share your weaknesses with your man or your child. Go inside to your navel point, concentrate on it, and you'll get your answer in seconds. The only thing that can make you a failure in life is anxiety. Anxiety comes from the fact that your sense of achievement and sense of timing conflict...Learn to listen to others calmly and yourself quietly. The moment you don't listen to yourself, you will naturally become anxious. If you don't develop your personality so your presence will work, your words won't work either. Your presence should convince a person that he is talking to a goddess."

Men often enjoy silent companionship; they don't feel the need to talk about everything in detail. (Of course this is another generality. I know there can be exceptions.) In most cases, if you tell a man you have a problem, he will immediately try to offer a solution. On the other hand, tell the problem to a woman, and her first instinct is to sympathize—at length. Men want solutions, women want sympathy. So that's what they give; men give solutions and women give sympathy, and neither gets what they want!

THE PEANUT HOUR

Understanding the nature of women, and their need to talk, Yogi Bhajan introduced the "Peanut Hour." He told us that it has been a custom in India for years. Women get together in mid-afternoon, to drink tea, eat peanuts, and talk.

But, here's a warning, do not, I repeat, do not *complain* about your husband. If you need help to work out differences, then find one very trusted friend or personal counselor. Keep any differences or marital problems strictly between wife and husband, and never, ever argue in public (or in front of your children). And, of course, that goes for men, too. You need to work out your stuff in private, through respectful and considerate communication. That means you *listen* to each other, take responsibility for your own feelings, and always speak with words that are kind. Thinking before you speak is a wise habit to cultivate.

WHY MEN LOVE WOMEN

A man doesn't love a woman because they have great sex. He doesn't love a woman because she's a good cook or a wonderful mother. All these are important, but the fundamental reason a man *loves* a woman is because "she can take him to the experience of his expanded infinite self."[17] This is not necessarily a conscious desire on his part, but it is there, deep in his being, and a woman who can inspire him, ease his stress and strain, and help him relax, will surely be his beloved forever.

Well, you may say, what about the woman's stress and strain? She may have been working equally hard all day; she probably still has to handle a big part of the household chores, so what about her need for comfort and relaxation? My apologies to my women readers, it's just not the same. Yogi Bhajan explained over and over:

"People who have the idea that a woman is a weak and frail creature do not know what a woman is. A woman is sixteen times[18] stronger than a man."

The Teachings of Yogi Bhajan

WHAT A MAN NEEDS

A man needs his wife to be a comfort, a support, the "pillow" on which he can rest his head at the end of the day, and download his worries and problems. Whereas if a woman is upset and emotionally disturbed, she should find someone else to tell her troubles to, instead of trying to turn her husband into her psychologist. No matter how stressful and exhausting her day has been, even if she has twice as many problems, a woman still has the capacity to provide nurturing. Woman is, after all, the cosmic "mother." She is the *Shakti*, God's power in manifestation.

Believe it or not, it makes a man feel insecure if his wife shares her insecurities with him. Insecurity is the main flaw in most of us women. When a woman is upset, the whole setup is a mess. Her negative vibration can poison the atmosphere. On the other hand, if she can rise above her insecurities, and use her feminine power, her patience, her compassion and her intuition she can create a home that is a haven of peace and tranquility, a place of comfort, refuge, and joy.

Smile a lot, and laugh together frequently. If you don't, you're missing out on the joy of sharing fun with someone you love, and without laughter, life is no fun and marriage is no fun—and it should be!

WOMEN SEEK SECURITY

While a man seeks a woman's support, a woman wants her man to provide protection and security. She may be a black belt in karate, but the kind of protection a man's strong electromagnetic field can provide is an unspoken, subtle power. See the section on "Methods for Men" to learn a yogic technique for strengthening a man's electromagnetic field. And yet, when all is said and done, a woman has to find her greatest security within her own being.

*"The joy of a male and female relationship is their friendship, the flow, the communication, the talking, name it anything you want, it can exist when you can avoid confrontation with a man, although ideologically you may be totally in opposition. It is possible. It is practical. There is only one point when you will fight....Out of **insecurity**. In the total life of a woman there is only this one word; if that does not exist, you exist. You will only fight, you will only destroy yourself, you will only destroy the relationship when you are insecure. It is a positive truth. Unfortunately a man can never give you security. Your security lies in your spiritual realm, in your spiritual consciousness, 'I am - I Am,' 'I am the Grace of God.' "*

(Women in Training VI: "The Oriental Woman" 1981 Yogi Bhajan)

GODDESS OR PROSTITUTE?

Yogi Bhajan didn't pull any punches. He said very bluntly that a woman in America has only two choices; she can either be a prostitute or a goddess. Purity in a woman is an incredibly powerful virtue, yet sadly it is seldom valued in today's promiscuous society. Women "take on" karma whenever they have an intimate emotional or physical exchange with a male, adding his imprint to the arcline[19] that runs from breast to breast (men don't have this arcline). This adds to the layers of memory that cover and dim the divine light within.

A big help for any woman, married or single, who wants to manifest her inner goddess, claim her power as a woman, and let her radiance shine, is to recite the Grace of God affirmation/meditation every day. *(See Chapter 11: Yogic Technology to the Rescue.)*

WOMAN'S POWER

It is a fact, whether we like it or not, the major responsibility for the success of a marriage depends upon the woman. As Yogi Bhajan proclaimed, "Woman is 16 times more powerful than man." Maybe she can't physically lift the heaviest weights, but her emotional and psychological impact on her husband is tremendous. A woman can really ruin a man, undermine his self-confidence and virtually emasculate him. Many women have done so, as history notes. On the other hand, the old saying, "Behind every successful man, there is a woman," still holds true today.

Women have the power to uplift and empower their husbands. And the good news is that elevating your husband not only serves to improve his feelings of self worth, but will automatically enhance his appreciation of you, thus making your own life happier. Don't we all want to spend time with people who make us feel good about ourselves, and do nice things for them?

FOUR PATHS TO LIBERATION

According to ancient teachings, to reach union with God, a man has only one option. He has to perfect himself through his own yogic practices. But a woman has four ways to achieve liberation. She can:

1. Do her own personal practice to reach a state of Yoga.
2, Give birth to a hero, a saint or a giver.
3. Serve a spiritual teacher.
4. Serve the God in her husband.

I know that last statement may seem outrageous in this day and age. But serving your husband doesn't mean you become his slave. It means you do things to make him feel loved and appreciated. Whether it's cooking his favorite meal or giving him a foot massage, you use your power to encourage and support him mentally, emotionally, and spiritually. When you love a man, you enjoy doing things for him, not because you have to, but because you want him to be happy and feel well cared for. Most importantly, when the wife sees in her husband the god-like man he actually is inside, she upholds him in her own mind and heart and reflects that back to him. That's not always easy to do. Yet it is easier to see the God in him if she determines to turn him into a saint. How does a woman do that?

Well, first of all, she keeps up with her own spiritual practice, no matter what. Hopefully, her example will inspire her husband to do the same. Of course, she never, never nags. Secondly, there are specific mantras she can use to elevate her husband's consciousness and turn him into a saint. In particular, Yogi Bhajan recommended reciting the *So Purkh* section of *Rehiras*,[20] eleven times a day while praying for him. There is a wonderful personal report[21] about the transformative power of this mantra. Yogi Bhajan calls it "a woman's special worship," saying:

The woman who will learn this shabd by heart and recite it will
never have any difficulty as far as men are concerned.[22]

MAGIC WORDS: GURU RAM DAS' ADVICE

I doubt if many wives today would heed the wise advice given by Guru Ram Das to his daughter before her wedding. But, if you think about them, the three statements he suggested can prevent, avoid, and solve any argument or conflict! But it depends on a woman being able to get her ego out of the way long enough to see the benefit, and recognize that the end justifies the means. Of course, as stated before, a woman should never give an inch when it comes to standing up for her principles, and maintaining her grace. But in cases of minor disagreements, these words advised by Guru Ram Das have been known to calm troubled waters.

"You're right."

"I'm sorry."

"It's the Will of God."

Remember, even if you win your point, you've lost something even more important. You've lost his good will. A wife can never win an argument with her husband, because the male ego bruises easily and may never heal. Losing makes a man feel emasculated. Do you think he's going to think kindly of the person who inflicts any indignity on him? With the strength of humility, the power of persuasion and the sweetness of surrender, a wise woman manages to maintain her grace and the integrity of the relationship. Most things that couples argue about are trivial, and not worth fighting about anyway. So, before you get into a fight, step back and decide what you really want as the outcome. "Winning" is usually not worth the loss of affectionate goodwill and the disruption of harmony in your home.

Yogi Bhajan often said, "God lives in cozy homes, not in crazy homes."

DIVINE MOTHER

Every female creature was intended from birth
To manifest the Universal Mother, nurturer of all mankind—
Fulfilling a sacred role as a goddess on this Earth,
—Does that concept blow your mind?

With yogic mastery and knowledge of cosmic law
Yogi Bhajan set out to transform "chicks" to "eagles," he said
He taught us the meaning of Shakti power
And how not to be exploited by men.

He spoke of the noble and graceful woman—
Concepts never outdated or obsolete—
With understanding of her divine nature
A woman becomes complete.

Whether she has children or not, each female has a unique role
In what is called "Lila"—God's Infinite play
Whether she's a housewife, a lawyer, or a CEO,
Noble women can impact the world with Shakti power today.

Virtues give invincibility
Purity gives beauty and inspiration—
Through her meditative projection
A noble woman can uplift a nation.

CHAPTER SIX

AH-MEN

MESSAGES FOR MEN

"Man is born of woman and you cannot deny that. However much you get it together in life, you owe it to that woman who carried you and made your body for 9 months and who taught you in the first 3 years the very basic things of walking on this earth and talking. So, all desires, enterprises and goals are focused on woman. You have sprouted from a womb, one half of you (the left side) is polarized female and you seek fulfillment in sprouting again in a woman. If you can, you will find your way into every womb on earth. You learn about yourself through being hurt by a woman. The thing to do is to respect every woman and try to increase her grace."

Yogi Bhajan

"Without woman you are not complete."[23]

"MAN TO MAN"

Whereas Yogi Bhajan devoted weeks and years to educating women, he taught only nine short courses[24] specifically for men. Someone asked him:

STUDENT: How come our men's courses are only two days and the women's course is six weeks?

YOGI BHAJAN: This is because the women need more rest than the men. In this country, woman has been so abused, so misused, and so much negated that it takes us about two months to get them together and create them together so that we can send them back super-positive. That's the motivation of those ladies' courses. When they go back we want them to go as super-positive and to keep going so that there may be less hassle in life.

"You have to understand that the most important, the most time consuming, nerve-consuming, intelligence-consuming, most creative job on this planet Earth is to raise a child to be a saint, and perfect. Few people appreciate this. ...

"We want the woman to be so strong basically; so creative, so intelligent, so compassionate, and so giving that she can handle this child-raising situation totally. This will take years to accomplish. That is why I ask of the men—I even call them personally—that they send their wives to ladies' camp." *(Man to Man 4)*

At another time when asked about the emphasis on teaching women, he explained that women are far more complex than men, and it required far more time to bring about the transformation of consciousness that was needed. He said that the effects would automatically impact and benefit the men in their lives. He worked to develop powerful, graceful women, who would be able to inspire, encourage, and support the success of their men, as well as bring up children to be, as he put it, "saints, heroes, or givers." In other words, excellent, independent, spiritual human beings.

He told the men, "There are certain qualities, certain calibers, certain constitutional differences, which have to be understood in dealing with a woman."[25]

THE SUCCESSFUL MAN

To be successful, a man has to be in harmony with the universe. That means he is able to align his life force with his destiny. Then his intuition guides him, not just his ego or his intellect, and he becomes a magnet for opportunities for success. No matter what challenges he faces every day, or how intense the pressure of his work or profession, he can maintain his balance and be secure in his sense of self.

How can a man evoke this inner strength and maintain his higher consciousness? Meditation. He has to go deep within himself and establish communication with his own highest self. Meditations that activate the pituitary gland, balance the hemispheres of the brain and/or strengthen the nervous system are especially valuable for men to practice.[26]

Specifically, meditation on the sound current of *Wahe Guru (Wha-hay Guroo)* strengthens the relationship between a man's arcline[27] and his pituitary gland, the master gland of the body. As for yoga postures, Archer Pose is highly recommended.

It builds the nervous system, improves not only physical endurance but also enhances a man's projection of strength and self-assurance. Archer Pose[28] works to develop courage. *(See Chapter 11 for more "Methods for Men.")*

There are three secrets of success. God has given you reason; God has given you emotion; God has given you feelings; you can express very clearly what you feel to somebody, but do not break anybody's heart, and do not break your trust. You can't force anybody to trust you. You have to win trust and you can only win it if you have the character and the courage to win it. And you can only win trust when you can give; you can never win when you take.

These are the three secrets of success Yogi Bhajan taught:

> *Never let down yourself,*
>
> *Never let down anybody.*
>
> *Never conspire to let down a living being.*

"Don't say anything against anybody to anyone; don't listen to negativity against anyone; and don't act negatively.[29] You will be free of all problems."

WHAT WOMEN REALLY WANT

"…Women want saints, heroes and givers.[30] That which they want to produce,[31] they want to have.

"Let me sum it up: They want a sexual saint. Nothing less and nothing more can satisfy them. You have to be a leader in three fields: spiritual, mental, and physical, in that order. Problem with you is your physical comes first when actually it (should) come last."

"Through your conduct (which is one thing very important to a woman), you should not behave as a drama and should not behave as a trauma. Both will not work. This is what a woman hates. Woman is a drama herself, trauma herself. Equal poles reflect, opposite poles attract. When you behave like a drama and a dramatist and 'traumatist' you lose a woman. Relate to woman as a simple, intelligent, man of your word."

Yogi Bhajan understood that women want to know if a man is intelligent and if he is compassionate. He said she wants him nicely dressed up, neat and clean. That's her nature; she likes it. It doesn't matter whether she herself is neat and clean, but she wants him to be. And she wants to be able to brag about that man for something. For example, how intelligent he is. If a man doesn't give her something to brag about, he is going to lose her.

No matter how independent a woman is, she wants to feel that her man can give her the security that he can provide and protect. "Her comfort with you as a man is that you can protect her, you can provide for her social grace, mental stimulant, spiritual compassion, and that you are a man of your word. A woman knows that if you are a man of your ego, the days of your marriage or relationship are numbered. You can stretch it, but it won't work."

HONOR YOUR WORD

Once a woman knows in her heart that you are a gentleman, and thoroughly a gentleman, there are no problems. One thing that a woman likes most is that you are a man of your word. And best of all, she knows that you have somebody 'higher up.' It may be a God, it may be an angel, a guiding angel, it may be a teacher, it may be a spiritual path, or it may be some spiritual tenets. Once she knows you have somebody higher than you, she feels secure and safe. These are the virtues which man has to relate to, to have a virtuous relationship with a woman in grace.

"Handling a woman harshly is inviting unavoidable trouble, and she will get to you. Trouble is only started by conflict and conflict between the areas of life is the conflict of the egos. To create a conflict of interest with a woman is to create a difficulty in your own life…." *(Man to Man Part 4 "THE MULTIPLE MAN")*

"Every relationship has a motivation. In business the purpose is to make money. Money is equivalent to security in business. In an intimate relationship, the purpose is to get out of loneliness. All sexual relationships have one purpose: to get rid of loneliness. All the rest is hodge-podge. Even sexual intercourse in itself is an expression of trusting each other, or letting each other trust that 'we do not believe in loneliness.' That's all it is. In all political and other relationships, the motivation is power: who controls whom.

"Do you understand these motivations? One is security. The second is to fight loneliness (man is a social animal). And the third is power. It is to these motivations that a successful man applies the art of creative dialogue."

"As a man there are three faculties that you must have: wisdom, humility, and the desire to serve…Humble means approachable, easy to communicate and talk with… and the third is that you have the desire to serve, that you are sincere in the purpose of service. Can you remember all this when you talk to a woman? That will enable you to use creative dialogue."

FANTASY OF THE PERFECT WOMAN

Most boys create a fantasy of a "perfect woman." If he wants to carry out his intention of making a success of his marriage, by the time a man becomes a husband, he needs to acknowledge and confront that childhood vision of the "perfect woman." As a mature adult, he has to recognize that vision was only a fantasy. Then he can establish, accept, and appreciate a realistic relationship with the female polarity. A man may think that like Pygmalion he can change a woman, and mold her into his fantasy of the perfect woman. Yogi Bhajan says[32] quite bluntly:

"…It's the greatest fault on the part of a man to think that he can change a woman… You can never change a woman. To think so is your biggest fault, your worst direction, and a totally wrong challenge for a man to take. Nothing is a greater waste of time, waste of life, and waste of energy. Don't make a project out of a woman. If you want to change anybody, the project must be to give yourself grace."

When a man works on himself to grow and change, his woman will be challenged and work on herself to try to match up to him.

"SIXTEEN TIMES" SCIENTIFICALLY EXPLAINED

"Woman has a kind of sensitivity. Her aura has more antennae than that of the man. Woman has sixteen more antennae per square millimeter, which is called 'electromagnetic antennic vibratory effect.' Woman's aura is much thicker than that of a man's. She can make you feel. Very few men have the quality to make you feel, but the majority of women can.[33]

"Woman is very intellectual. She is sixteen times more intellectual, and sixteen times more compassionate, and sixteen times more patient than a man, by construction of the two beings…. God made it that way. If she is convinced with a compassionate heart, with an Infinite reason, she can tolerate the worst with you. The circumstances under which a man would leave you, woman can go through it without even grumbling. That is the inherent quality in her."

MONEY: YOURS, MINE, OR OURS?

"When a woman makes her own money, it should be treated exactly the same way as the money YOU make is treated. That's what is called a joint account. The household must be run by a joint effort, not with the attitude that 'it is your money,' and 'it's my money.' The moment you create 'yours' and 'mine' you have already ruined the household. These are the mistakes…and that is why the rate of divorce is going higher and higher. Money is a medium; money is what money does. Money is not mine or yours. Money is ours. And it is very beautiful if you are very honest with a woman in these areas."[34]

WHEN DOES A BOY BECOME A MAN?

We say a boy starts to "become a man" when his beard starts to grow. Yes, and that is because the hair that appears at a certain stage of development (usually about when his voice changes) is God's clever way of covering the moon center[35] in a boy's chin so that he will no longer be primarily under the influence of the lunar, feminine, or mother energy. (Hair absorbs solar energies, thus neutralizing the lunar effect.) Various religions have ceremonies and procedures that acknowledge when a boy is considered to have become a man.

It takes a real man, not just a male of a certain age, to take on the responsibilities of marriage, to be mature enough to make a lifetime commitment!

RUDYARD KIPLING[36]

IF

If you can keep your head when all about you
Are losing theirs and blaming it on you;
If you can trust yourself when all men doubt you,
But make allowance for their doubting too;
If you can wait and not be tired by waiting,
Or, being lied about, don't deal in lies,
Or, being hated, don't give way to hating,
And yet don't look too good, nor talk too wise;
If you can dream—and not make dreams your master;
If you can think—and not make thoughts your aim;
If you can meet with triumph and disaster
And treat those two imposters just the same;
If you can bear to hear the truth you've spoken
Twisted by knaves to make a trap for fools,
Or watch the things you gave your life to broken,
And stoop and build 'em up with wornout tools;
If you can make one heap of all your winnings
And risk it on one turn of pitch-and-toss,
And lose, and start again at your beginnings
And never breathe a word about your loss;

If you can force your heart and nerve and sinew

To serve your turn long after they are gone,

And so hold on when there is nothing in you

Except the Will which says to them: "Hold on";

If you can talk with crowds and keep your virtue,

Or walk with kings—nor lose the common touch;

If neither foes nor loving friends can hurt you;

If all men count with you, but none too much;

If you can fill the unforgiving minute

With sixty seconds' worth of distance run -

Yours is the Earth and everything that's in it,

And—which is more—you'll be a Man my son!

CHAPTER  SEVEN

CHALLENGES IN MARRIAGE

HOW TO SPOIL A MARRIAGE
Pour just one little drop of lemon juice into a glass of milk and the whole thing curdles and turns sour. Similarly, there are three ingredients that can turn your marriage sour. They are the three "C's," Compare, Compete, and Complain.

▸ COMPARE

This is a sure way to ruin your marriage. Your husband or your wife can't possibly measure up to some real or imaginary ideal you have in your mind, so if you keep on

comparing, both of you will be miserable. Accept the fact that every person has a collection of faults, and though we work on them and try to become better "day by day in every way," as Dr. Emil Coué recommended, realistically, no one is perfect! You have to be able to know and feel and think, "I love you, I accept you, warts and all." (Though I don't suggest saying that.)

Every man has a deeply imbedded concept of his "ideal woman"—and very rarely can any wife measure up to that. Similarly, women have the fantasy of the perfect man. And, in both cases, it is just that, a fantasy.

▸ COMPETE

Marriage is a partnership. It's not a competition. Each person brings certain strengths and certain weaknesses to the partnership. To make it a success, you want to support and compensate for the other person's weaknesses. (And kindly overlook them if possible.) That brings balance to the team, and makes it stronger. Maybe one of you is really good at finances and can easily balance the checkbook; the other likes to cook. It doesn't matter which one does what, but use common sense when figuring out how to share responsibilities.[37] Yes, we know there are fundamental differences in the nature of each gender, the Sun and the Moon characteristics, but don't get stuck with stereotypes when it comes to the daily chores. Be on the alert so that neither of you is a control freak or trying to dominate the other, because then the marriage is heading for trouble.

▸ COMPLAIN

This is the third, but not the least, of the terrible trinity of marriage breakers. Got a problem, something that you really need to get off your chest? Something he's doing —or not doing? Something she's doing or not doing? Well, okay. Find a kind and courteous way to gently remind, suggest, or request. And take personal responsibility for your own feelings and reactions, don't "blame." And unless it's a terribly important major issue: once is enough. Don't keep harping on the same thing over and over. That's called nagging. Women are notorious for doing it.

ARGUMENTS: DON'T HAVE THEM

Never abandon or compromise your basic values, but if and when there are disagreements over little things, wise is the woman who lets the man have his way. Let him choose the restaurant or the movie. Richard Carlson wrote a popular book, *Don't Sweat the Small Stuff*. The title says it all and is good advice for married couples. Making a mountain out of a molehill is a waste of energy.

Of course when it comes to the major decisions, where to live, rent or buy, if and when to have children, you need to plan and work it out together. These are things you should discuss and agree on before you get married.

Discuss, but don't argue. The fact is a wife can never win an argument with her husband. Even if she makes her point and gets her way, she's lost. Because the man will feel diminished. He will resent her for that feeling. So, don't have arguments, have discussions. Still, even in a discussion, things can get pretty heated up, so be sure to keep plenty of water on hand—drink it to cool down (don't throw it!).

NEUTRAL SPACE

When you have to work out issues where you disagree, keep some ground rules in mind. Don't assume the worst. Remember the legal phrase, "innocent until proven guilty—beyond a reasonable doubt." What I'm saying is, give your partner the benefit of the doubt and remember what you're discussing is an issue of "we"—not "me" versus "you." If he/she has said or done something hurtful, start from the premise that it was not intended to hurt. Going back to Communication as the key to harmony, look at conflict as an opportunity for growth where each of you is willing to speak openly, honestly, and respectfully. Doing a meditation together before a discussion can be a very helpful way to neutralize any conflicting energy so that you don't approach the topic as adversaries but as a couple trying to solve a mutual problem. When all is said and done, remember, come what may, to use the touchstone of your spiritual commitment. If both partners put God and Guru first in their lives, together they can resolve and solve any problems they meet.

INTERFAITH MARRIAGE

Religious prejudice and persecution still exist worldwide. For centuries religious fanaticism has caused wars. Someday, God willing, the time will come—hopefully when we finally, fully enter the Age of Aquarius—that no religion will create boundaries and barriers of animosity among people. Meanwhile, we have to face the fact that in today's society, differences of religion can be a deal-breaker. The factor of religion needs to be seriously examined by couples contemplating marriage.

If we are willing to define marriage in its highest sense, as the Highest Yoga—with the divine potential to amalgamate and merge two souls into one—then having the husband on one spiritual path and the wife on another is going to require some fancy footwork. That's not easy when there are fundamental differences in basic beliefs. Men and women have been known to remain happily married and maintain different tastes in sports, entertainment, clothing, and even politics. Democrats and

Republicans can peacefully co-exist in a marriage (though they'd be wise to avoid discussing politics – especially at the dinner table). But when a husband and wife are strongly committed to different faiths, the challenge to the marriage is enormous. It's especially difficult to bring up the subject of religion when people (especially young ones) have "fallen in love" and there's that chemistry of attraction that can happen no matter what religion the other person is. When the hormones kick in, the brain goes to sleep and doesn't want to have to think about the practical challenges they will face as a couple.

I have to admit that it's not impossible for an interfaith marriage to work, but religious differences add a huge burden to an already challenging relationship. So, please, before you get too involved, learn more about this topic.

How committed are you each to your faith? How actively engaged are you in your religious community? What are your daily practices? Will your relatives accept your marriage to someone of a different religion? Will you be treated with icy reserve or given an openhearted welcome?

You may agree that because there is only One God, ultimately the Goal is the same, no matter which path you're on. But let's look at this idea more closely from a practical standpoint.

Some religions worship God in human form; some do not. Is God personal or impersonal or both? Some faiths have rules about food and others are identified by special clothing. Devout Catholics do not eat meat on Fridays; Khalsa Sikhs never cut their hair. Observant Muslim women and orthodox Jewish men and women always cover their heads in public.

Where will you spend holidays and which ones will you observe? Are you going to go your separate ways on separate days to church or mosque or synagogue or temple? Are you going to try to convince or convert your spouse?

HOW TO RAISE THE CHILDREN?

Do you agree on how your children will be raised? Are you sure you won't change your mind later when it's time for choosing between baptism and circumcision? Later on will it be *Bar Mitzvah* or Communion or *Amrit*?[38]

In a desire to be universal and all embracing, one may say that children should be exposed to all religions. I agree that they should learn about all religions and be taught to respect the rights of all people to follow whatever path they choose. But it is the daily living example of their parents' same religious practice that confirms and strengthens a child's own personal identity..

One of the most important responsibilities you will have as a parent is to give your child a deep sense of security and a strong sense of self-identity. How is that going to work when Mom and Dad have different belief systems about God, the Creator, the very foundation of all life?

When a child has parents practicing different religions, it can set up conflict, competition and confusion in the child's mind. If the child leans toward one or the other religion, he/she will feel they are choosing one parent over the other. So both parents need to make sure that they talk to the child explaining clearly the issues and differences in a way that enables exposure—but does not create conflict. And as for the child choosing a religion, at what age? What level of maturity is needed to make that choice wisely?

I believe to truly experience a religion, to drink from its wellspring of inspiration and guidance, you have to dig deep, and keep digging in the same place.

"Religion is not a documentation of rules and do's and don'ts. Religion is my own life conducted by me. It is my conduct, my personality, and my reality. It is my truth, my light, my prosperity, my happiness, and my totality." Yogi Bhajan

Husband and wife remaining side-by-side practicing the discipline of this highest yoga together requires compromise, flexibility, and above all tremendous mutual respect and continuous, sincere support for each other. This example of harmonious living sets the pattern for children to follow when they become adults.

GROUNDS FOR DIVORCE

Fed up? Can't take it any more? Is that you screaming, "That's it!"

Hold on a minute! Divorce should be the last resort, not the first choice. While spousal abuse, alcoholism, or drug addiction are extreme circumstances in which divorce may be the only solution, for most marital problems or conflicts there are other options to explore. Before you call the divorce lawyer, have a talk with your minister, priest, rabbi, or professional counselor. Hopefully that person has a yogic, spiritual understanding of life and marriage and is familiar with your religious values and lifestyle. Speaking with family and friends isn't always the best idea, because they are biased one way or another. What you need is a neutral, informed third party to help you find a way to save your marriage. And don't underestimate the power of prayer and positive affirmation to help solve the problems you are having. Faith moves mountains.

Yogi Bhajan explains marriage counseling:

"There are two types of marriage counseling. One is to counsel for the marriage's sake and the other for the individual's sake. It depends on the counselor's attitude. If a counselor works for the marriage, he will counsel them together or put them together and find out what is separating them. But when a marriage counselor works for the individual's sake, he may split a marriage, which could not have otherwise been split.

"Divorce is very messy. Afterwards is when real marriage starts: children, child custody, abuses, yes, no, trying to become friends with the guy you divorced. God, it is a hell. 'Hail the hell' is divorce."[39]

ALTERNATIVES TO DIVORCE

When there are serious problems, there's the simple expedient of creating a temporary separation. If you can get away from each other for a while you stand a better chance of getting a fresh, clearer perspective. "Going home to Mother" isn't what I'm suggesting. Rather, it would be ideal for the wife to go to 3HO's Women's Camp (KWTC) for a couple of weeks. Here's where male/ female issues and problems are discussed and understood in a safe supportive atmosphere, with Yogi Bhajan's teachings providing the insight and technology to help women discover their inner power and learn how to manifest it in the most positive way.

As you will read in Dr. Sat-Kaur's article,[40] unresolved sex or money problems are two of the "biggies" that cause divorce.

Whatever the problem that has brought either of you to the brink of divorce, look for other solutions before you give up on your marriage.

SEX AND SPIRITUALITY

"Sex has everything in it when it is performed consciously by two people as an act of merging the physical, mental, and soul bodies together. Then those two bodies become one simple unit. At that moment, nothing stands between those two. This pure merging causes those individuals to become one with everything."[41]

SEX

A great sex life is one of the perks of marriage. It's an important component of a successful marriage. Enjoy it! It is the expression and manifestation of genuine affection, love and caring between husband and wife. Married love includes a natural desire to merge, to become as close as possible to the person you love, not only physically, but also mentally and emotionally. It takes time to develop a mutually satisfying and compatible sex life. Hopefully you'll experience that. Patience pays.

You need to be able to communicate and talk about sex openly and comfortably. You can find important and specific information about sex, what, when, and how to communicate about it—depending upon factors such as your age, previous experience, and background, in the books listed in Sources and Resources. Also see Yogi Bhajan's unique and classic lecture, "There is Nothing in Sex and Without Sex There is Nothing," on page 52.

DOUBLE STANDARD IS A FACT

Sexual intercourse is the most potent and lasting of all karmic exchanges—and that is what makes sex before or outside of marriage so damaging, especially to a woman. Women have an extra arc line (part of her aura)—from breast to breast, that men do

 not have. It is thus that a woman retains a permanent karmic "imprint" of any male with whom she has sex. That's why through the ages, prostitutes have been looked down upon, not because of any moral judgment, but because prostitutes carry a huge load of karma they've taken on from being intimate with so many different men.

"Marriage is a spiritual identity; not just a love affair between two people."

Yogi Bhajan

IT'S IN THE STARS

Here's a little Astrological tidbit for those who are interested: In the horoscope (the blueprint diagram of your karma), what we mistakenly call "love" affairs, are shown in the Fifth House, which is the House of Romance (vs. "reality"). Marriage, however, is the domain of the Seventh House, the House of Partnerships. So the dynamics of a relationship between a man and a woman, especially those who have had premarital sex, is bound to change when they marry. From a yogic standpoint, love comes from the fourth chakra, the heart center, where- as lust is a second chakra activity, the energy center associated with the sex organ.

"Physical intercourse is called 'the bridge of seven constructions.' You can elevate your physical, mental, and spiritual body seven times over if it is an intercourse of mind, body, and soul —if it is sacred, if it is worthwhile. Otherwise it is the dumbest thing to do."

Yogi Bhajan, Aquarian Wisdom Calendar, 2005

SEX IN THE CITY AND THE UNIVERSE

The peacock fans his feathers
And parades to attract a mate
Deer butt their antlers, testosterone raging
When a winsome doe is the bait.

It's a human urge, an animal instinct
To seek and mate and multiply
Mother Nature built this in
To propagate the species
So the race will never die.

The planets in orbit, attracted by the sun
Held in check by their spinning force—
All part of the polarity game—
The name of the game is "Sex"—of course.

Ads for everything from refrigerators to cars,
Cigarettes, champagne, and booze
Claim they'll enhance your success with the opposite sex
(So girls sacrifice feet and spines—wearing sexy spike-heeled shoes.)

We confuse lust with love
Though they're not the same at all
There's nothing evil about attraction—
Just don't let it make you fall.

Romance and reality are opposite poles
Still we "fall" in love over and over again
Hormones start raging when the age is ripe
And boys think it means that they're men.

Casual sex in recent years
Has become an accepted trend
Except, my friends, it's a basic fact
The law of Karma doesn't bend!

A man may merrily, carelessly scatter his seed—
In his psyche there's barely a ripple.
The woman, however, carries a permanent imprint
In the extra Arcline she has (it runs from nipple to nipple).

Every encounter, every affair, leaves a permanent mark—
Sometimes a scar—on each woman's history
It's not a question of moral judgment—
Karmic consequences are not a mystery.

In the cosmic scheme of things
This may come as a surprise—
The ideal woman has just one sex partner,
Her husband (!), for her entire life.

So, marry, my children and enjoy a full sex life
To neither abuse nor misuse is your goal—
See the God in each other; then revel in pleasure
Ecstatic merging of two bodies sharing one soul.

You say you're not married? Then what can you do?
How do you manage that urge to merge?
Practice Sat Kriya and Frog Pose (a lot!)
Help second chakra energy upward surge.

Yes, Kundalini Yoga is the yoga for householders
Designed for people with husbands and wives and careers
Be master of your emotions, your energy and your Self
Not the slave of the body's dictates—throw away your fears.

Movies and novels (at least they used to) create the illusion
That if your chemistry works, you'll live "happily ever after"—
The tragedy is that it's Divine Union the soul really seeks
And that's an entirely different matter.

Hatha yogis used to sit in caves, afraid to eat garlic[42] or see a female form.
But despite their pledge of celibacy, they often had x-rated dreams.
The ideal management of the basic sex drive is not denial,
But intelligent education and communication (it's not so hard as it seems).
Talk to yourself and your partner (that's called communication)
Learn about Kundalini Yoga, (valuable education)
Decide on your goals, what you want out of life
Then take steps to achieve what's already in your heart.

"THERE IS NOTHING IN SEX AND WITHOUT SEX THERE IS NOTHING"

(Excerpts and commentary on a Yogi Bhajan lecture. By SS Guruka Singh Khalsa)

IN THE HOUSE OF NANAK, the life of the householder is the highest spiritual path. Through creative union, couples function in the sixth sense, which unites them beyond time and space. This process of amalgamation between couples is real, and it must succeed now and forever.

Yogi Bhajan teaches us that there is nothing in sex and without sex there is nothing. This seems at first not to make any sense. Like many of Yogi Bhajan's teachings, it is a purposely provocative statement. Let's take a closer look and try to understand what he is getting at.

In a yogic marriage, sexual communion becomes an instrument to raise your consciousness and take you to divinity. According to Webster, "communion" means "sharing, exchanging, common possession, and spiritual union." Sexual communion is consciously, willingly, blending with your partner in a pure sexual merging that is a spiritual act. Two become one in the sense that each represents the other, each can speak for the other, each lives for the other, and each stands for the other. It is a bonding that exists beyond this physical world, and it is a bonding that is eternal.

Sex has everything in it when it is performed consciously by two people as an act of merging the physical, mental, and soul bodies together. Then those two bodies become one simple unit. At that moment, nothing stands between those two. This pure merging causes those individuals to become one with everything. It is without ego. If one can know that two can amalgamate to the oneness, then one can know the secret of oneness. By knowing the secret of oneness, one can be one with the One universal existence. Sexual communion is that divine. If you allow your ego to become involved, the experience is lost. For example, if a woman thinks, "I have to have intercourse with him because he gave me a necklace or he brought me flowers," then it becomes a business of selling character values for benefits. Sexual communion is a willingness in which two identities want to amalgamate. The amalgamation of two egos brings out a neutral, new personality.

In the scriptures it is written:

Dhan pir eh naa aakhee-an bahaii ikatay hoe,
Ek jot do-eh mooratee dhan pir kahee-ai so-eh.
"They are not said to be husband and wife who merely sit together.
Rather they alone are called husband and wife, who have two bodies and one soul."

Understand that when you make an alloy you take two elements and put them together. The alloy cannot be separated. That is what love is, that is what marriage is, that is what life is, and that is what good luck is. When a male and a female merge together, it is a pure act in spiritual unison. It prepares them to merge consciously into the infinity on that day when they depart from this earthly world. Sexual energy is a powerful, vital energy that is continually generated within the human body. It offers a vehicle for fulfilling a divine destiny, and therefore requires the most reverent mental, physical, and emotional preparation. During the merging of two, feelings are aroused to the point of worship. *Shakti* (feminine energy) worships the *Shiva* (male energy), and *Shiva* melts like the early morning nectar into her. Then there is a unity.

The act of sex is very powerful, very energetic, encouraging, inspiring, and it widens the consciousness. It does everything right when it is done with the right intention, the right environment, the right circumstances, and with the right person. But when these things are not right, then it can create psychological problems, bring out childhood traumas, and lead to guilt, insecurities, anger, and fear. When sexual behavior is selfish, it becomes nothing but a tragedy. When one's life is motivated by unconscious sexual feelings, when one is unaware of the consequences of thoughts and behavior on the self or others, when one creates a world based on selfish sexual actions (lust), attachments, or perversions, then there is nothing that is good or real. Such behavior becomes destructive to the self and others. Sexual union is a vehicle that can create an evolution of energy unto heights of ecstasy. But when it is wrongly performed in abuse or obligation, or is misused, it can be detrimental to the same being; so in both ways, it is an energy.

This is a very tricky subject. Nobody can afford to be lustful and as such disconnected from the needs and joys of the partner. But everyone must love. Without love, you can never find your life, and with lust you can never enjoy life.

Yogi Bhajan says: "Sexual communion cannot happen until a woman knows her divinity and manifests the faculties of the moon as the man manifests the faculties of the sun. Then a couple can understand and appreciate the waning and waxing of each other. What happens otherwise in unconscious sex is an unfulfilling, draining, and mechanized exercise. You put a lot of coal on the fire, you create a lot of steam, the locomotive moves, it creates the sound, and then there is a release. That is the end of the situation. It is a purely physical act, and this leaves the couple drained of their energy.

"Sexual communion takes you beyond the five physical senses, into the sixth sense, which is the total amalgamation of your five senses at a higher frequency. We call it the 'sixth sense' or the 'sex sense.' The human body can emit a sexual scent that can affect any person. Once a woman becomes attracted by the scent of a man, she may contain the man in her psyche, and there is no power on this earth that can separate them. The human scent is very powerful.

"The sixth sense is completely intuitive. Each one feels the other. Sexual energy between couples travels in a circle from a woman's Third Eye or her sixth chakra, over to a man's sixth chakra, then down to his second chakra, over to the woman's second chakra, and then back up to her sixth chakra. Sexual energy travels in this cyclical motion, which is controlled by the woman. A man has to understand that a woman has all of her sexual organs internally, while a man's are external. It is a within and without situation. Her entire mechanism is inside. A man's entire mechanism is outside. So he must learn to play more to bring her out. That is fair sex. Otherwise, it is unfair sex. It is also 'ladies first,' meaning ladies should reach their tidings (climaxes) first.

"You must understand that in life there is nothing but energy. Matter is a form of energy. Matter cannot be destroyed, nor can it be created. It can only be changed. So your physical body has energy that can be transformed into matter, or matter in your body can be transformed into energy. During sexual intercourse you play out this energy exchange. There are many kinds of physical intercourse i.e. intercourse through verbal dialogue with the tongue, intercourse through seeing with the eyes, intercourse through listening with the ears. But the question is, 'does the couple consciously understand the frequency of communication and the flow of energy?' Until a couple consciously moves the energy, with the sixth chakra in unison with the second chakra, they do not know sex at all."

When sex is only a physical impulse, it does not encompass the entire experience because the couple does not exchange the energy of each other's psyche, which connects the electromagnetic (energy) fields and produces the experience of one soul in two bodies. This exchange can bring happiness, better communication between the couple, and the amalgamation of two psyches in which neither is an individual.

As Yogi Bhajan explains: "Couples can have sex and produce children, and they can have a sexual release, but that release brings only temporary satisfaction. We call it "rupture sex," i.e. sex for the sake of sex. Lay your number, lay her up, and go away. This makes a man non-communicative, and any guilt derived from the act can also make a man unproductive. It is a serious handicap for males and females in this society.

"Let us take an example. Suppose a boy starts when he is just 13 or 14, scattering his seed among as many girls as possible. Then he marries when he is 26. So by that time for 12 years he has been following this behavior, and it has become habit. He may want to change, but it is almost impossible. Here in the West, girls come from the same training school. Both have been trained to have quick sex and depart. For years men in the West have been trained to be selfish, and then later on in marriage they are supposed to become very homogeneous and cooperative.

"Realistically, people go right on behaving as they were trained. "You know, she has the habit of sleeping with Joe, and she has been with Robert and Henry ...' up to 11 or 12 people. Her psyche carries an imprint on her aura of each man she has been with, and this makes it difficult for her to concentrate at all.

"And he also has the habit to be with 32 girls—so he is going through his mental movie. Both are in their mental movies and neither knows how to be for the other, or to feel the other, or live for the other. These old habits are some of the main causes of every known trouble in the sexual life in this country.

"We usually act as the by-products of circumstances, environments, and actions that constitute the habits that make up our behavior. Habits are embedded in the subconscious, and on the average our subconscious guides about 60% of our actions. Prejudice and bias guide about 25% of our actions, and only 15% of our behavior is conscious. Our sexual failures, our social failures, our family failures, our individual failures, and our human failures are failures because this is how we have been trained.

"We can look to an alternative training. In the yogic scriptures life has been divided into four phases or 'ashrams.' First is 25 years of celibacy when a man may retain within himself all the semen for growth and knowledge. After 25 years of age, man and woman may marry and have children, up to 50 years old. From 50 to 75 years, one may travel the earth with his or her partner, sharing teachings and wisdom from experiences in life, re-establishing contacts from youth, and inspiring people to become healthy, happy, and holy. From 75 to 100, one may sit and meditate and wait for the call to quit. This is how 100 years of life have been divided in the normal prosperous growth of a human being.

"If somewhere within a human, the ego gives up and the will of the Infinite prevails, then one can become healthy, happy, and holy and consistently experience a sacred sexual life. Every human being has a choice and the power to change.

"These days many marriages are dissolved between the age of 36 and 45. That is a period when marriage has become boredom, and everybody wants to look to new values. You must be aware that nobody looks to new values, and there is no such thing as boredom."

Marriage is an institution that cannot get boring because it is a continuous battle against time and space. How can a thing become boring when you have to exert every minute of your life to keep going?

"DEAR YOGIJI"
AQUARIAN TIMES MAGAZINE – SUMMER 2002

"Dear Yogiji" is a section from the Kundalini Yoga magazine Aquarian Times.
Here are some of Yogi Bhajan's answers to questions on relationships and sexual bonding.

Q: *Would you explain the blending of the auras?*
A: When a man and woman have intercourse, their Yin and Yang energies merge, and their auras blend; it is a purification. The two people become a different third person. A woman is especially sensitive to the blending of auras. If she blends her aura with one person here and another there, her aura is imprinted, and she cannot hold on to her identity. Her energy is very sensitive, and this merging of auras can have a very destructive effect on her. She can become emotionally weakened. This is very prevalent in our culture. For woman, sexual freedom should not mean sexual exploitation; it should mean sexual preservation, choice, and reverence. On the other hand, if there is love, commitment, and respect between the two people, intercourse can have a very positive effect on her. She will feel creative, expansive, vital, and secure.

Q: *As a woman, what can I do to lose the imprints of past partners?*
A: Everyone has an arc line—call it the aura. But a woman has an additional arc line between the breasts. Ordinarily the imprint of every sexual relationship a woman has is never erased from this arcline. However, if you do Sodarshan Chakra Kriya[43] it can definitely clear the imprint(s) out. This meditation has been done for the last 3000 years. It will also help you.

Q: *I want a relationship with a man, but my fears have been sabotaging me. How can I overcome this fear?*
A: If you want to get rid of your fear of men, then do 31 minutes of long deep breathing (daily). Although it may take a little time, it will heal this subconscious block.

Q: *What is the impact of stress on sex, and what can we do to have good sex under high stress?*

A: Fill a tub with warm water up to the navel point. Remember the water should not be too hot or too cold. Sit in the tub and do 15 minutes of Sat Kriya.[44] Then lie down in the tub and relax. Afterwards come out and you will be able to enjoy sex. It works.

Q: *Is there a best time of day to have sex?*

A: Avoid sex between 3 a.m. and 6 a.m. Because of the position of the sun with the earth, it is a very sensitive time of day. Avoid sex within three hours after eating, after physical exercise, when the woman is deeply menstruating, when you are under stress, and when you are not in a secure place. Any other time is fine. It should not be done in haste and worry. You must be brought to the point that you relax and thereafter sleep.

Q: *Then what can a man do about horniness?*

A: To feel horny is not a sin or wrong, but if one knows how to invoke the meditative mind, which raises the energy up, one can become totally creative. Horniness on the physical plane can manifest as sexual intercourse; on a subtler plane it can manifest as creativity. It is the same energy, used differently in different body centers.

Q: *When men and women approach middle age sometimes they experience a decline in sexual desire. How can this best be dealt with, both physically and emotionally?*

A: Sit together back to back and do Sat Kriya. Centuries of experience have proven couples remain together, very successful. It is also useful for couples going through calamities, indifference, and unstable environments. Two spines joined together in Sat Kriya can do wonders. I wish you all the success.

Q: *I have read that the Kundalini energy flows up the chakras in a spiral motion. When the energy goes down, does it also do so in a spiral motion?*

A: Yes, that is the route it takes. If the flow is free and open, it is great, but the problem is if the flow is limited or blocked, then the energy is only for maintenance. To keep the Kundalini energy in a rhythmic flow and allow it to settle properly in the chakras, Sat Kriya is the best.

Q: *What about sex during pregnancy?*

A: This is a controversial topic. Sexual energy is too intense for the unborn child. Once the pregnant mother is about four months into her pregnancy, intercourse should stop. Let her pray and be one with the growing child within her.

Q: *Does this mean that intimacy, affection, and touching stop?*

A: No, not at all. In fact, it is very important that mom and dad are very affectionate with one another. The parents' love is the most important thing a baby experiences in the womb. It can overcome the negative effects of many stresses and traumas.

SIKHNET YOUTH FORUM

The SikhNet website has a section where youth feel free to ask frank and personal questions about the Sikh view on many issues, including marriage and relationships. They can do so anonymously. Here is a real question that was asked June 1, 2005, as well as the answer from one of the moderators of the Forum.

Q: *What are sins for Sikhs? If I did have pre-marital sex would I go to hell or be reincarnated? I know you recommend having sex after marriage but if someone was to have sex before marriage would I be punished? I see sex as being natural as breathing. Bye.*

A: I am not going to answer you in a typical "moralistic" way. I am going to answer from a Yogic and consciousness perspective. When two people have sex the auras merge...you become one aura. It takes 7 years minimum for the woman to get the man's aura out of her aura, and some times it takes much longer. Sex is such a very sacred act that it requires a commitment in the relationship. Sex can penetrate the psyche of the individuals involved, especially the woman, on a very deep level. If sex is not treated with sacredness and commitment, both people can be hurt very deeply. For these reasons, it is best if sex is done after marriage.

Humbly, GTKK

CHAPTER NINE

PROFESSIONALLY SPEAKING

The following articles offer wise perspectives on the art of marriage from both the yogic and psychological points of view.

CHALLENGES: "THE BIGGIES"

BY SS[45] SAT-KAUR KHALSA, PHD, ED.D. MFC, LPCC, LM

SS Dr. Sat-Kaur Khalsa is a psychotherapist and Marriage, Family, and Child counselor. She is in private practice in Santa Monica, California, and Santa Fe, New Mexico. A KRI[46] certified Kundalini Yoga teacher, White Tantric Yoga facilitator, and ordained Minister, she also serves as Secretary of Religion for Sikh Dharma. She specializes in relationships and personal growth. Dr. Sat-Kaur combines insights from her professional psychological training with deep spiritual awareness. She is the author of the book *Sacred Sexual Bliss*.

Relationships are an opportunity to grow and expand both individually and as a couple. Re-la-tion-ship: a ship about learning how to relate to one another. It is also statistically true that the two biggest issues in most relationships (if left unaddressed) that lead to divorce are sex and money.

The sexual relationship for most couples is a microcosm of the macro. That is, if there is a lack of mental, emotional, and/or spiritual connection in other areas of the relationship, the physical relationship tends to reflect these issues. What distinguishes a marriage from a friendship is the sexual component. A healthy, active sexual relationship is critical to the success and longevity of a marriage. If there are problems in this area, they need to be addressed and resolved sooner rather then later to keep the marriage connected and loving.

One of the elements that can help the sexual relationship tremendously is to keep courtship alive in your marriage. I often suggest to couples to have a "date night" at least once a week. The ground rules are that you are not allowed to talk about money, children, or schedules. One week the man is responsible for planning the date and the next week the woman is responsible. The idea is to engage in fun and different kinds of activities with each other (that don't have to cost a lot of money). Dinner and a movie are all right once in a while, but there is no real communication or connection watching a movie. It is so easy in a marriage to get bogged down with all of the responsibilities, that courtship and romance go right out the window. These components are extremely important in fostering a healthy, connected sexual exchange. This little "dating" exercise can make a huge difference. Try it. See for yourself.

If you want to see people's neurosis, talk about money. Most people are very private about this component in their lives. However, in a marriage, it is essential that both individuals not only know and understand their joint financial situation, but they also have equal say as to how their joint money is spent, saved, and used. I often suggest monthly or at least quarterly budget meetings about joint finances. If both people are going to be fiscally responsible, both need to know and understand what money is available, what expenses there are and what discretionary income there is if any. This area gets very complicated when one or both individuals have non-joint finances.

However, the key to solving challenges of all shapes and sizes in a relationship is the ability to communicate with each other. If you can talk to each other in such a manner that both parties feel heard, understood, and acknowledged, you can resolve almost anything. We are taught, particularly in the United States, in communication to "cut to the bottom line." That is, we give our conclusion without any explanation as to how we got there. In relationships, this kind of exchange is disastrous. I often suggest to couples to use a paragraph of explanation. Let the other person understand how you concluded what you did. Then your partner needs to acknowledge what you've said before responding. This kind of exchange between partners maximizes the chances of both individuals being heard and understood. Based on these components, most couples can resolve the majority of their issues.

Yes, relationships are complicated but they are worth the work. They are truly the richest opportunity for growth and change, transformation, and liberation. I wish you success in your journey.

KNOW YOUR INTENTION (OR REASONS VS. INTENTIONS)
BY SS SHANTI SHANTI KAUR KHALSA, PHD, MFT[47]

SS Dr. Shanti Shanti Kaur Khalsa is the Founder and Director of the Guru Ram Das Center for Medicine & Humanology based in Espanola, New Mexico. A Sikh Minister and KRI Certified Kundalini Yoga teacher trainer, Dr. Shanti Shanti lectures and teaches internationally. Here's her article:

Recently I was having lunch at a TGIF's in the Chicago Mid-way Airport on a layover from New York City. In the booth behind me were four women in their late twenties or early thirties, clearly friends and obviously single, discussing, "Why get married at all?"

I couldn't help but overhear:

"The reason I would get married would be to have children. I want kids and I don't want to raise them myself."

"I'll get married when I'm finally tired of dating and want to settle down."

"I would get married because I don't want to be alone when I am older."

"I'll get married when I find a man who can support me. Everyone knows that men make more money than women. And if the marriage ends in divorce, I will get a better settlement if he makes good money."

The conversation continued with what qualities make a good husband, the paltry selection of marriageable men, and time running out on their biological clocks.

I would have liked to be able to share the thought with them that when we finally do marry, we may know our reasons, but we may not know our intention.

Intention is not the same as reasons. Reasons change and it is part of the evolution of a relationship that they do. In a long-term marriage, partners recognize over the course of time that the reasons they got married are not the same reasons they have stayed married.

Growing up we have an image of marriage, what it would be like, what it would fulfill. Along the way, we make decisions about what we do and don't want in a spouse and we form strong opinions about why—or why not—to get married.

Every seven years marks a change of consciousness, every eleven years brings a change of intelligence, and every eighteen years a change in life. If the reasons for marriage are not periodically evaluated, renewed or replaced, the relationship may not match up to the changes made by the marriage partners. For example, if a couple gets married because they have so much in common, what happens to the marriage when they discover how different they are from one another?

When reasons for marriage do not evolve with the changes the husband and wife have made, there is conflict in the relationship at its foundation, and the couple may not stay together.

Intention is more deeply rooted than reasons. It is more enduring and does not usually change over the course of time. When you identify your intention in marriage you shift the frame of thinking from what you want to get from marriage to what you can bring to marriage. Intention sets the direction and stability of the marriage and allows trust to grow.

In a healthy marriage, what spouses trust is the intention of each other. Intention is the base and strength to face the challenges of life together.

Often couples come to marriage counseling to find common ground on finances, sex, or parenting; to learn skills to resolve disagreement or conflict; or explore techniques to improve communication. In reality, these methods take us only so far and are not sufficient to maintain change.

When couples are in conflict, at odds, in pain, not getting what they want, it is helpful for them to stop first, and remember and reconnect with the intention of the marriage before addressing the issue at hand. Once this understanding is renewed and shared with each other, it is not that much further to finding and forming solutions. Keeping that conscious connection to the intention of the marriage strengthens their ability to maintain the solutions agreed upon.

So how could the women lunching at the airport move from their "reasons" to marry to their "intention" in marriage?

The woman whose reason for marriage is to have children may find her intention is to nurture a family whose strength and security carry through generations.

The woman whose reason for marriage is to settle down, may set her intention to create stability and continuity, to move closer in relationship through any difficulties.

For the woman whose reason to get married is to avoid loneliness, her intention for marriage may be to bring depth, genuine communication and coziness to her life through the marriage.

The woman whose reason for marriage is financial support, may have as her intention to trust the Divine Unknown in all matters and to serve her marriage.

Reasons may get you married; but it is a deep, clear and shared intention that keeps you there.

"Marriage is an institution in which two individuals of opposite polarity decide to build a cozy environment which is called home, and through thick and thin of time, they adjust their behavior. Without adjusting their behavior, no marriage is possible."

Yogi Bhajan, *The Man Called The Siri Singh Sahib*

ANGER MANAGEMENT
SS DHARAM DEV KAUR KHALSA, LPCC, MFT

I asked my friend and neighbor specifically what advice she gives when counseling couples about anger issues. Here are some of the ideas she shared with me. Thanks, Dharam Dev!

How you handle anger is one of the single most important factors in the health, longevity, and satisfaction of your relationship. Without essential anger management strategies and skills it's not likely that your relationship is going to be happy or can even survive in the long term.

Anger is a perfectly normal emotion. Everybody gets angry sometimes, it's just a matter of degree from minor impatience to blowing a fuse. We all have *agni* or fire energy as part of our makeup.[48] We need the fire element to digest our food, and to give us courage. It's when the flames rage out of control and are liable to burn down the house that we're in trouble. The important thing in a marriage is to understand what triggers anger, and if those "triggers" cannot be prevented or avoided, learn how to handle the anger that results.

People tend to get angry when they feel they have been injured in some way, mistreated, or opposed (i.e. "don't get their own way"). It's a natural instinct to want to fight back. But that isn't necessarily a solution, and can do more harm than good—especially if you lose control.

Anger can be so powerful that it takes over our sense of reason. It's as if the brain shuts off. When a person's anger gets out of control, they often say and do damaging things they will truly regret later.

Think about your own anger response patterns. Do you raise your voice and yell? Do you get physically abusive? Break things? Try to identify the things that have made you angry in the past, and remember what you did when you were angry. Then plan what to do instead, if a similar situation occurs. What positive action can you take instead of flying off the handle, having a tantrum, or storming out of the room?

This is called Planning Ahead.

Here are some suggestions for Self-help:

Choose one or more of the following techniques to practice daily so you can apply them later when/if you find yourself in a potentially anger inducing situation:

▸ Long Deep Breathing (Slowly repeat a calming word, such as "relax" while you are doing long deep breathing.)

▸ *Sitali Pranayam*[49] *(yogic breathing to cool down – see page 102)*

▸ Close your eyes and visualize a calming, relaxing place or experience. (Use your memory or imagination)

▸ Go for a walk.

▸ Write a letter about your anger—for your eyes only, don't keep it. (Maybe burn it? That's a positive use of the fire element!)

▸ Drink some water to cool down.

▸ Read an inspirational book.

▸ Do a yoga set that has stretching, relaxing movements.

Those are some good ways to deal with your own anger. What about when your partner gets angry?

▸ Remember safety first (get out of harm's way if necessary)

▸ Stay calm

▸ Physically remove yourself from your partner if he/she tends to get physically abusive

▸ If safe:

▸ Sit calmly, listen and acknowledge his/her feelings

▸ Say soothing calming words in a low, slow voice

▸ Offer water or a snack (water puts out fire! And maybe the person's blood sugar is low, and a little food could help!)

▸ Do yoga, meditation, *Sitali Pranayam*, or long deep breathing together.

▸ Remember that people are sometimes too emotional at that time to be able to discuss what's happening. Instead, try comforting them or just giving them some space.

▸ Don't compete with their anger or it can escalate. In other words, don't answer fire with fire.

▸ Set aside a special time each week to brainstorm solutions to problems/frustrations/challenges you may be having as a couple. This can cut down on future confrontations.

It's important to remember that you can't eliminate anger all together. Inevitably there will be things you will each get angry about, but you can learn to control your responses to avoid causing pain and destruction in the relationship. By working patiently together you can support and nurture the enduring and loving companionship of marriage.

KEEPING UP FOR 33 YEARS
SS GURU TERATH KAUR KHALSA PHD

SS Guru Terath Kaur Khalsa PhD is the author of *The Art of Making Sex Sacred* and *Dying Into Life: The Yoga of Death, Loss and Transformation*. Also coming out soon, *You Don't Have to Be a Pretzel—Yoga Done on a Chair and Bed*.

Marriage is the foundation of most societies and cultures; it is so compelling that most people have tried it at least once. When done successfully it brings more fulfillment and joy to the participants than anything else and when not done successfully it brings tremendous heartache and pain.

No couple ever goes into marriage thinking that they will ever fall out of love, become bitter and end up yet another divorce statistic. In addition to the trauma the couples experience, those who suffer most are the children. In my capacity as a licensed counselor, District Judicial Courts send me cases where parents cannot work out differences. Sandwiched between the feuding parents are the innocent children who unfortunately often carry these scars for life.

From what I have seen counseling couples and families, there are two problems. One, couples contemplating marriage get caught up in romance and don't do enough investigation before they say, "I do." And second, once married, couples give up too easily.

I encourage couples thinking about marriage to get to know each other on a deep, honest level, asking themselves and each other as many questions as possible. Below are a few examples. Create your own questions according to your situation.

- ▸ What is important to you?
- ▸ What are your goals in life?
- ▸ What do you want to be doing 5, 10, 30 years from now?
- ▸ Where do you want to live?
- ▸ How do you feel about having children? How many?
- ▸ What is your parenting style?
- ▸ What's your perception about who raises the children? One parent or both? What will that look like?
- ▸ What do you physically and emotionally need from each other?
- ▸ What are your sexual beliefs and needs?
- ▸ How do you feel about sharing your feelings and listening to mine?
- ▸ How do you relate to your parents…and mine?
- ▸ What role will the parents-in-law play in the marriage?
- ▸ How do you feel about my working or not working?
- ▸ Who is the breadwinner of the family – one or both of us?
- ▸ What financial needs and expectations do you have?
- ▸ How will money be handled?
- ▸ How important are material things to you?
- ▸ What's your bottom-line of what you want in the way of a house, car, boat, summer home, education, etc.?
- ▸ How do you feel about either one being away from home for business?
- ▸ How important is religion/spirituality to you?
- ▸ What spiritual/religious expectations and needs do you have of your self and of me?

Of course it is very important that both people be totally honest in their answers. Also, besides asking questions, spend time and observe each other in various situations and settings.

If something is not the way you want it to be before marriage, you can assume that is the way it is going to be after marriage…or worse. The worst thing you can do is to assume that everything is going to be okay after you're married. Never think that you can change the other person to be the way you want them to be. I encourage couples to refrain from sexual intercourse at least until there is a decision and firm commitment to marriage. When two people have sex, the auras merge, making it almost impossible to be objective and neutral about the situation.

Once married, couples give up way too easily. I warn couples, "As much as you are in love today, there will be times when you will hate each other." No one wants to believe me. One time I went to Yogi Bhajan with a complaint about my husband. Confident in my grievance, I thought for sure he would sympathize with me. Instead, he just said, "Keep up, endure each other, and build on the positive."

My husband and I have been married thirty-three years. Over the years, I have tried to follow Yogi Bhajan's advice to me. Life is about change. Times change, feelings change, circumstances change, but if there is commitment, caring, and compromise, marriage can endure, and become even more endearing to both parties. These are some tips I have learned along the way:

- When faced with a conflict, meditate first; discuss later—when I'm clear.
- See the God and goodness in my husband, instead of the imperfections.
- Stop the negative thoughts with a mantra.
- Keep my heart open.
- Make time to be together.
- Keep a sense of humor and have fun together.
- Keep my spiritual practice strong.
- Live my mission in life.
- Allow him to be who he is and me to be me.
- Serve him with a smile and an open heart.
- Keep my needs in mind, while fulfilling his as well.
- Have a spiritual practice together…Venus Kriyas[50] are great.

‣ Take time for my self.

‣ Make time for sex and keep it meaningful and fun.

‣ Get away together.

Marriage is hard work. It is the hardest yoga of all. Over the past thirty-three years, all of my garbage has surfaced. I had a choice. Either I could face it myself, blame my spouse or run away. I'm so glad now that I chose to stay and face myself. Through all the trials and hardship there has been much joy and the dessert has been fulfillment. I am grateful that I followed Yogi Bhajan's advice and just kept up and kept going.

"IT MUST BE LOVE, BUT LET'S BE SURE"
(EXCERPTS FROM THE LOS ANGELES TIMES MAY 21, 2005)

Staff writer Ellen Barry wrote:

"Couples these days are undergoing counseling to see whether they should get engaged. In the divorce-heavy South, churches recommend it.

"Increasingly, couples are seeking out "pre-premarital" or "pre-engagement" counseling—the opportunity to sit down with trained advisors to examine, dispassionately, whether their love is a passing fancy. This step, though still rare, is on the rise across the country. In the South, the most religious and divorce-prone part of the country, many churches have begun to recommend it.

"In seminar halls or living rooms, dating couples practice the art of the painful conversation, face cold realities about sex and money, and catalog childhood traumas that might leak into their married lives. They examine printouts summarizing their psychological make-ups and the weaknesses—sorry, "growth areas'—of their relationships.

"It may not be the kind of love story found in Hollywood movies, but premarital counseling responds to a yearning for a more reliable path to marriage. Using tools from social science, it aims to prepare the partners for conflict, prevent unions based on blind impulse—and, ultimately, reduce a divorce rate as high for religious couples as for other Americans."

"If someone's going to learn how to drive a car, you're going to take classes, read the manual…You're not going to just jump into it. Unfortunately, that's how a lot of couples approach a romantic relationship."

"… A movement is afoot to rethink the structures around marriage. Lawmakers in Arkansas, Louisiana, and Arizona have passed bills creating "covenant marriage," a contract between bride and groom that limits grounds for divorce to extreme conditions including adultery and abuse. Lawmakers in Florida, Arizona, Tennessee, Maryland and Minnesota have passed bills offering a financial incentive for couples who attend counseling or marital education before they marry. In the conservative heartland, couples counseling, offered at many churches, has become ordinary.

"Some have looked hard at the way Americans choose husbands and wives. In his influential 1997 book, *I Kissed Dating Goodbye*, Joshua Harris, a home-schooled evangelical Christian, attacked the short-term relationships of adolescence and young adulthood as a perfect training ground for adult divorce.

"Harris popularized the alternative of 'courtship,' which constrains the couple's freedom to be transported by emotion. In courtship, parents would arrange meetings and group activities until the couple was ready to marry.

"That idea of courtship has never quite taken off, …parents love it, in essence, it's giving them control—or more control—over their child's relationship. Singles are saying that's not working. … recommends the more palatable alternative of pre-engagement counseling."

• • •

Author's Note: According to Eastern tradition and culture, couples do not go out on dates alone. They are never without a chaperone, and marriages are very often arranged.

Yogi Bhajan used to say:
"In every date there is a pit."

CHAPTER TEN

WHEN YOGI BHAJAN SPEAKS
VOICE OF THE MASTER

Those of us who were blessed to sit in Yogi Bhajan's classes and listen to him speak in person found his words elevating, transforming, challenging and powerful, yet always loving—even when he shouted! We knew he cared about us. His marvelous voice would go from gentle cajoling syllables to stentorian tones that vibrated deep into our psyches. Sometimes after a particularly confrontational statement, he would say "Why are you so serious?" And then he would chuckle! He taught values, virtues and ideals and made them seem desirable and even attainable. Every word hit home.

Written transcripts simply do not do justice to his spoken words. As much as possible in these articles I have tried to preserve the flavor of his speech patterns. He coined words; he had a unique rhythm often employing an unorthodox sentence structure and his words were so effective that each person felt he was speaking directly to him or her. In all of Yogi Bhajan's lectures on Marriage, he emphasized the same concepts over and over, undoubtedly so that they might actually sink into our "stone" heads, the same way a drop of water can eventually, after centuries of hitting the same spot, make an imprint in a rock.

Following are some of Yogi Bhajan's profoundly insightful and forthright discourses on marriage. May you read them over and over again and engrave them in your hearts.

WHAT IS MARRIAGE?
Yogi Bhajan • July 15, 1984

You all have to realize what a marriage is. Marriage is not an easy path. Marriage is a life. Marriage is not a ceremony; marriage is God.

Marriage has not been understood by the Western world at all. It was understood by the Eastern world but it is forgotten there too. So at this time, the institution of marriage is in total limbo. People do not know what to do with it; people do not know what to do without it. So what we have found out via the media is that marriage then divorce and divorce then marriage is a continuous process. But actually, if we all understand what marriage is, then perhaps we can do better.

Marriage is an institution of willingness, in which two identities want to amalgamate. It's an amalgamation of two egos to bring out a neutral new personality. What is the advantage of it and what is the disadvantage of it? When this amalgamation happens, then divine power in the psyche starts to function. Without that, people are individuals and they will only yell and scream at each other and goodness will never come in that home. It is a granted fact.

Marriage brings happiness. It's an amalgamation of two psyches. And when these two psyches are amalgamated, neither one is an individual. There is no question of he and she. That's it. There is no loss, there is no gain and there is no bank account.

"This is what my husband said," does not exist. "I will ask my wife," does not exist. If there is no confidence that the husband can speak on behalf of his wife and the wife can speak on behalf of her husband, they have not yet married. If this is the commitment, that the husband cannot commit on behalf of his wife and the wife cannot commit on behalf of her husband, they do not know what commitment is. To make an alloy, you take two elements and put them together. The alloy cannot be separated. You can boil it, you can form the alloy into a liquid, you can totally burn it, but once it becomes an alloy, it will totally keep its own quality, own quantity, own weight, own molecules, own electrons, protons and neutrons, and own combination.

Whatever made brass doesn't matter. Brass has its own faculty, own quality, own weight and own property.

And that is what love is, that is what marriage is, that is what life is, that is what good luck is. There are no two opinions about it when a male and female merge together. That's why we do it before God. That's why we do it before Guru.[51]

We bring together friends and relatives, the mother and father stand up, and they give the hand of the daughter. The daughter merges with the man. Parents give the *palaa* (shawl) to the man and he gives the shawl to his bride. And we sing the song, *Palaa Tainde Lagee*. Once you give the *palaa*, let your head go, but that offer, that support must not go. And once she holds that, she must let her head go, but not let her hold go. And that is what marriage is.

If you think you know what marriage is, and you say, "We'll never be emotional, we'll never fight with each other," then listen to this. If you really look at the marriage, there is nothing to fight about....

"I am intelligent, she is a duffer; she is intelligent, I am a duffer. She is rich, I am poor; she is poor, I am rich." All this has no meaning in marriage. Try to understand marriage. It is a simple, unique situation. Where amalgamation takes place, a new metal comes out of the two. A new ego comes out of the two. A new identity comes of the two. And it is forever. It is not only for today and not tomorrow.

Try to understand. Everything can come to an end. Even life can come to an end. But one thing even God cannot end: the desire to be one in each other. This desire even God cannot take away. To be one with one is not the desire over which God has the control. This is one desire before which God has surrendered, God has obeyed and God has become little. The Almighty GOD, the All-pervading God, has become humble before those who have an utmost desire to become one with the One. Once they become one with the One, they manage God.

AN IDEAL MARRIAGE
Excerpts from Yogi Bhajan lecture • July 22, 1976

Love starts after marriage and lasts up to death. Marriage is an institution that depends upon honoring the Word. That is why the Scriptures say, "Whosoever honors the word of his marriage is honored in the court of the Lord." The Word of God is nothing but a test of two individuals—a given promise. The Guru says,

> *Bhai jeena dee pakareeay sar deejay bheheena chareeay.*
> "Once you give your hand to somebody in the relationship,
> let your head roll off but let not your hand go."

The institution of marriage can be anything in ritual. But in reality it is an honest, living word of two individuals. And it must be lived unto God, unto the last breath, through time and space, come what may. If this is missing, everything is a sexual, physical, emotional relationship for temporary convenience. It is mental prostitution. So don't misunderstand the institution of marriage and its cause and effect.

The best course for a human relationship is that each couple, when they get married, should take a vow to do their job and play their part right. Whether your parents and relatives approve of it or not, it is important to be respectful to them. Every marriage can become successful if both partners play their part honestly.

In marriage dark days will come. In reality marriage is an institution where two individuals decide to build a cozy environment, which is called home. Then through the "thick and thin" of the times, they are constantly adjusting their behavior. Without adjusting the behavior, no marriage is possible. People feel that divorce is a way out when two cannot live together. But no divorce has solved the problem. Basically divorce creates problems.

Everybody has faults. You divorce a man with 26 faults but then you marry a man with a set of 27 other faults. What's the point? Broken hearts, broken homes. God lives in cozy homes, not in crazy homes.

The question arises: What is an ideal marriage? An ideal marriage is a way of life in which a husband and wife compromise to face the time and space to stay together for the security of their own life and their children.

WORDS AT A WEDDING
Yogi Bhajan • July 6, 1986

Marriage is not what we understand; actually marriage is what we are trying to understand on this earth. For generations and generations, through every religion mankind has tried to create an institution of marriage. Sometimes we live it, sometimes we don't. The practical reality is that marriage is the most misunderstood institution ever created by man.

Some people think marriage is just to produce children. Others think it's just to run a household. Some feel marriage is to get rid of loneliness, and some say, "How can I go out in society as a single man? I need to have my better half with me, so I must find somebody."

If you look into the very inner urge of the human being, there is always one thing or the other making people want to marry. If you go very deep in the scripture, it says, "When a man is young, he has the 'juices,' so he wants to multiply himself." In analyzing the subconscious we say that he wants to produce his own image—and you know in that image he sees God.

He falls in love, gets a woman, produces this, produces that... well, there are books on it. You can read them in your spare time. But the fact is, marriage is not a merger,[52] marriage is reconciliation between two people for their own better good.

I am not going to tell you that marriage is a very soft, sophisticated, beautiful thing. I think marriage is getting together to get it together forever, to face this earth, whatever it gives you, bad and good. The problem is that we expect too much good from the earth, and under the weight of that good we all die, it's such a weight that we can't carry it.

The polarity of life is that two people come together before God. It's very unfortunate when people get a divorce—they never come before God! They only come before God to get married. That's funny; they go to the court to get a divorce, that's strange. Normally I think it should be that you come before God and accept each other and when you accept each other, then you keep on accepting and never stop. That is meditation. That is marriage. That is religion. That is God. That's everything you want to know.

I am not saying that you will not sometimes be indifferent to each other. I am not saying that you will not have different opinions. I am not saying that you will not have clashing arguments. I am not even saying that you will not get sick of each other. But in spite of those momentary, temporary earthly feelings, if you just remember that you accepted each other before God, then these things will dissolve.

When there is no God in our life, then there is trouble. Because God in unison-ness is such a powerful thing. In your freedom of life, in your independence of life, in your excellence of life, whatever you want to do, do it for God's sake but don't misunderstand that both of you went before God one day, bowed four times and accepted each other. The very essence of one's human honor is that two people accept each other in public among relatives and among friends. What more honor can there be but to honor it forever?

In my fifty-seven years I have never understood why we divorce each other, why we fight with each other and why we are indifferent to each other. Why can't a human being created in the image of God create harmony? I have not understood it. I have heard the arguments. I have counseled people who say, "Oh, our chemistry doesn't work." I don't know what they are saying. They have every excuse in the world. It's common knowledge that everybody has an excuse, but the common truth is that everybody has the essential potential possibility to merge with another.

Now, this is how I look at marriage: if you cannot merge with each other (that's one unit of human being to another unit of human being) then how can you merge with God? Then you are the biggest hypocrite practicing spirituality. It doesn't mat-ter whether you are a Sikh, a Muslim, a Christian, a Buddhist, an anarchist, a social-ist or a communist. You may be French or German or Italian or Japanese, and you can say anything you want, but the fact is that if you cannot just accept another human being as God, and part of God, and you cannot merge, then I don't think you understand what this life is all about.

My trouble is that somehow, basically, I believe in one fundamental thing: woman is the grace of God. All my troubles started from that day when I started saying "I am going to make every 'chick' an eagle."

My belief is, that in this universe, we don't need atom bombs and we don't need Star Wars missile defense and we don't need anything like that. Wars will never decide mankind's future. Never! War at home will not decide the future of the house and war in the street will not decide your social future. War at each other—throwing plates and throwing your breakfast pancakes at each other—will not decide your economic future. None of this can decide your future. Only one thing will decide the future, *one thing*: if one woman… one! (I am not asking for four and a half billion women—they say there are four and a half billion men and women on the earth), if one woman—with purity of heart and clarity of head, and one man with purity of heart and clarity of head can unite, can merge with each other and create one Christ-like child, create one Guru Nanak-like child, create one Buddha-like child, which can bring peace to every heart. That is what will decide our future.

We need another Moses to lead us to the promised land of peace and tranquility. We need another Christ to give us the power and strength of peaceful coexistence. We need another Buddha who can still say the truth no matter what. We need another Guru Nanak who can see the infinity of God and still feel humble. That's all that we need.

To be very honest with you I am not worried. Normally I used to preside over marriages. I stopped doing that because some people came before me, promised themselves to each other before the Guru, and then they applied for divorces. I couldn't stand it. I couldn't understand it. So I have just retired myself from those kinds of things…

Marriage with a reservation, good or bad, is not marriage, and it never will be. It's my personal opinion, absolutely personal, that people who marry and have any reservation, good and bad, are not doing it right. Marriage is one proposition in which there is absolutely no reservation whatsoever.

THE STORY OF RAJINI

Today I'll let you know the story of the Rajini. The Golden Temple stands on this story. It is a story on which grace and fatherhood and the most healing part of Guru Ram Das stands.

There once was a wealthy *kardar*, a tax-collector, who had seven lovely daughters. Of these, Rajini was the youngest. Her father provided all of his beautiful, charming daughters with graceful environments, the best of teachers to cultivate their talents, and the finest in clothing and food. He gave them each much affection, and they were known for their beauty and virtue. But, he was very proud of his ability to provide so well for his family, and constantly reminded them what he had given them. In time, the *kardar* married his six eldest daughters to wealthy men of good social status. Soon, it would be Rajini's turn to be married.

One day, all seven sisters were together enjoying the gardens in the far side of their father's estate. On returning home they came across some saints in meditation. Rajini, entranced by the beautiful sound of them singing God's praises, decided to stay behind and listen. The saint sang the words of Guru Nanak:

> *Naanak junt upaai kai sunmaalay subhanaah.*
> *Jin karatai karanaa keeaa chintaabhi karanee taah.*
> "O Nanak, He who created the creatures takes care of them all.
> The Creator who created the creation, He takes care of it too."

Having listened and been uplifted, Rajini, in gratitude gave her fine jewelry as an offering to the saints, then returned home.

She was so elevated by what she had heard, she shared the words with her sisters. Upon their questioning after her jewelry, she told them what she had done. Her mother, on hearing this, angrily told her husband. He called all of his daughters before him and asked them who it was that had given them their food, clothing, and jewelry. He asked them who looked after them and took care of them. Rajini's six sisters answered that it was their parents who did all of this. Rajini answered that it was God who provided and took care of them, as He does for all of His creatures.

Her father was enraged. No matter how he put the question, nor how often, Rajini's answer remained the same. In his extreme of ego and anger he told her that he would marry her to the next man that passed in front of the window. His sight fell upon a leper who had somehow been brought to the village to beg for food. He demanded that Rajini be married to him at once. Obedient young Rajini had no choice but to marry this leper who couldn't walk, who couldn't eat, and who had open wounds all over his body. And so the marriage took place. Then the whole family took this leper, put him in a basket and put the basket on her head and said,

"This is the dowry and this is the farewell and never come back to us ever again."

Rajini said, "Can I have ten minutes in our house to say a prayer?"

The father said, "No, eight, cut it short, get out, that's it. You get out of here. I don't want to see you; I am sick and tired of you telling me that I do nothing for you and that 'God does everything.' "

The painful story is that Rajini did pray and in her prayer she said, "God Almighty I am very grateful to you. I am very blessed that you have given to me the man I deserve. My love for you is eternal and all I ask of Thee is that You help me to carry this responsibility with utmost grace."

Now you American girls sitting here who are married, and those who are unmarried, just understand that this story of Rajini is our root.

Rajini took this leper in that basket and then she realized that his wounds were so many, and the flies and other things were coming so heavily, that she asked her parents for something to cover him with. Her father refused and it is said that her mother took off her *chuni* (silk head scarf) and gave it to Rajini, whereupon the father beat her up. "You have no right to do that!" He yelled. Rajini covered her leper husband with that *chuni*, took the basket on her head and walked out of her parents' home. She started married life by walking from village to village, getting some food to eat for herself and to feed her husband. It's a true story known to millions of people and it didn't happen two hundred thousand years ago. It happened and it is verifiable. Each spot where she sat is there, alive and well, and the villagers still tell Rajini's story.

Finally Rajini, who was very thirsty, came to a pond where the nectar tank of Golden Temple of Amritsar is today. At that time it was just a very small pond. Under a Bir tree she put down the basket containing her husband, covered him, gave him water, washed his face, washed his hands and said, "Please be so kind as to stay here. I am going to the adjoining village to ask for some alms or food so that we can survive. Be peaceful in this basket." So Rajini left her husband by the bank of the pond and went into town.

As her young husband sat in his basket he saw something very unusual. He saw blackbirds come and dive into the pond and then fly out and their color had turned from black to white, like little angels. He watched this odd scene for a long time and then he thought, "Maybe I should try something." So he shook himself out of the basket and rolled himself right into the pond at the place now called *Dukh Banjhan Bir*. For that tree was there even then.

He dipped himself in the water and in moments he found himself totally healed. But he kept one finger out of the water. Here was his reasoning, "If she comes and sees me healed she will not recognize me, then I will show her this finger."

Soon Rajini returned with food and she saw a very beautiful young man, smart and handsome, sitting there and she said, "Where is my husband?"

He said, "I am your husband."

She said, "No, no, that's not true! Have you killed that unfortunate leper just because you want to have me? No way! I am married to him and I will defend my honor with my life!"

He said, "Calm down, calm down. It really is me. I am the same person. Don't you recognize my clothes?"

She said, "Clothes? You must have stolen his clothes."

He said, "No. I am healed. I went in the pond. Look at my finger. See? Now watch this." So he went and he dipped that finger in the water and it came out perfect.

She said, "No, no, no, that can't be! I don't believe it."

He said, "All right then. We cannot agree. I say, 'I am your husband' and you say, 'I don't believe you.' You say, 'My husband is a leper.' I say, 'I am cured. You saw my finger; it got cured. You don't believe it.' You are just being paranoid. In this town lives the saint, Guru Ram Das, let us both go to him and let him decide."

So they both went to Guru Ram Das and Guru Ram Das looked at them and told Rajini, "Rajini, this man is your husband and for centuries people have been trying to find this pond. We have already dug *santhok sar*. And now we will call this place Amritsar, the tank of nectar." And Guru Ram Das and the entire Sangat came to the pond where Rajini's husband had been placed in the basket and blessed the couple. To cut the story short, circumstances compelled the father and the mother also to come, whereupon they gave all their lands to Guru Ram Das, and there Rajini and her husband lived and ruled. It was within that area, then called *Chak Ram Das*, that Guru Ram Das started building the Golden Temple.

Now this is a very basic story of northern India. It is the story known by every Sikh and it's the story for every egomaniac woman who thinks that she has every right to have everything in the world and who doesn't believe that something that seems negative can actually be a huge gift.

Sometimes you do not have the nervous system to deal with life. But what is a spiritual life? If a spiritual life means that you cannot deal with negativity and calamities then where is your strength?

So basically, that is what marriage is to us. That is why we come before the Word of God and bow and take a vow to live together forever.

I think when two people get married, they do not live for each other. That's a wrong conception with which I have never agreed in the past eighteen years and I am not going to agree with today. You don't marry each other for yourselves. You marry and live for the children, whether you have them or not. You become the guardian angels of those innocent lives God brings into your life, and I think that's a very divine thing for every human being.

When I counsel you and you tell me "Well, our chemistry does not work. We are not together emotionally. We don't understand each other. He is not paying any attention to me. I am not paying him any attention." When you do not talk about those children, which you have just left in the care of some friend, I feel that you are very ignorantly blind and emotionally cruel. I believe that. I don't say so most of the time because I don't want to offend you.

I think people who are that naïve, that blind and that dark that they cannot see their own children, and have passion, kindness, compassion and feeling and grace to be like angels to them, I think there is something very wrong. Such people are worse than animals. I see birds making their nest, laying their eggs, hatching their little ones, protecting them, teaching them to fly and training them to be on their own. But in our own lives we forget all that. We fly away from our nests before even knowing we are going.

…Today I am asking you both to not feel great and to not feel little either. I am asking you both to understand the oneness between you two. For in that oneness, God shall bless you. I am asking you to lift yourself above your smallness. I am asking you to elevate yourself out of the myth of your body, your emotions and your feelings. Today I am asking you to dive deep into the totality of yourself and total yourself up. Feel that this is, this was, and only this shall be. Just remember that God never forgets anybody. We who walk on the path of God are tested and tortured. We are put on hotplates.[53] We are boiled alive. We are put through many tortures, and we have been crucified. But just remember, in the end we who walk on the path of God leave behind a legend. God is love.

I hope that the Minister now presiding here has to declare that you, in terms of the state laws and the federal laws, are married. You have completed your rounds[54] before the Guru and your marriage is complete.

Just one last line: It doesn't matter what happens, just remember this one thing, "When things are down and darkest, that's when we walk the tallest." Remember that one line. And at the end of the *Song of the Khalsa* it says: "We will die before we fall." That is marriage.

Marriage is not the fulfillment of your emotions, feelings, relationships and the raising of your juices. Marriage is to blend together in the oneness of God. With this I pray that you may remain married forever in essence and in reality so that you can understand the joy of it.

Wahe Guru Ji ka Khalsa; Wahe Guru Ji ki Fateh.
"The Pure ones belong to God, all Victory belongs to God."

MORE OF YOGI BHAJAN'S MEMORABLE QUOTES

Yogi Bhajan explained and emphasized the value and true purpose of marriage in many different ways, but always with the same basic message. Here are more excerpts from his lectures and remarks he made during weddings he performed as a Minister of Sikh Dharma and at Khalsa Women's Training Camp (KWTC).

"Marriage is a partnership of two beings of light who live by their intuition, understanding, and a common, genuine interest of well-being."

• • •

"You are a help to each other. The purpose of the relationship is to relay the help. Relay-tion-ship: relay the ship. Deliver, deliver, deliver, deliver. It comes exactly to that..."   (KWTC, June 29, 1988)

• • •

"...Look at Christianity, what do they say? 'If you adopt him as husband, and he adopts you as wife it's till the last day of breath.' Why don't you go to the same priest and see if he says, 'Now I break your breath and divorce you.' You go to the court of law to have a divorce; you don't go to the church. You get married in the church; you get divorced in the court. In the modern day, physical experimentation—to live together for purposes of emotional, social, and economic satisfaction—is called marriage and love. Actually, before God, marriage is one thing forever... When all is one and one is all, it is called love and when two persons decide it, it is called marriage."

• • •

"Why are there quarrels between husbands and wives? Because they have never tried to become one. They are still two who are living under one roof. They are still two who are sleeping in one bed. They are still two who are managing one home. They are still two; one is driving the car and one is sitting and sleeping on the side. But they have not yet become one.

"Marriage is when two become one. This is an institution in which we say we have invested a lot. Now I am telling you as Americans, so listen to this: If we cannot create an institution in which we create oneness of two individuals, then a child cannot be born with the caliber and intelligence to save the planet Earth…

"A frustrated husband and a frustrated wife can only produce a frustrated child. We create nine million frustrated children every year. Out of that, three million leave their parents and run away, three million are not successful, and three million are hassling. This country produces nine million children who understand the need to achieve, but who cannot be happy. Nine million people are added to this civilization. Every ten years, nine million frustrated people will bring twenty-seven million divorces. It is a mathematical thing, because each frustration must be tried thrice. Nine multiplied by three is twenty-seven."

• • •

"Where are we going to go? We want to be one with God. We want to experience God. We want to see America happy. We want every American to be happy. We want a home. We want security. We don't want law and order problems. We want, want, want, want, want. There is a long list. The list is taller than the Washington Monument. But we never do anything to achieve it. To achieve a goodness of God is to not have frustrated people.

"What we do now is patchwork. We counsel each other, 'This is because of this, that is because of that. You get out of it this way.' You get out, get out, get out of where? Ultimately somebody says, 'There is no place to go.'

"There is one place to go, to which you both have gone today, and that is: you both have to amalgamate with each other. I can bet on that, if you amalgamate honestly, good luck will come around you as you have gone around the Siri Guru Granth four times.[55] Happiness will come. Goodness will come. Grace will come. Everything will come because God never likes frustration.

"This institution of amalgamation, oneness, which Guru Nanak talked about is called "Ek Ong Kar." You are the creation of the One, and therefore you are One."

• • •

"Through bad or good, Keep Up! That is the real key to success."

• • •

"Now listen to this one thousand year old theory. It always works. A "fe" who does not merge into a male cannot be a "female." A *wo* ("wo" means greatness) who cannot contain the man, cannot be a "wo-man." You can try any other method you want—western, eastern, northern, southern, central, Chicago theory. Use anything. There is only one thing and that is that *amalgamation is forever*. Good and bad, great and small, all of it is in one pot now. In this you will find peace and tranquility."

• • •

"The one act to perform is for a man and a woman to merge as one. If from this minute they merge as one, they amalgamate now, they shall succeed. Success is not anywhere else. By manipulation, nobody has ever succeeded. Human manipulation is ineffective over divine psyche. By lying you can escape a situation, but you will never be respected. By corruption you can fulfill your emotional and commotional body, but you will never be trusted. There are certain laws of life. And those laws are responsible for the earth's rotation and for the continuity of life. So that is also God."

• • •

"There is a lot to learn and there is a lot to understand. But there is one thing I want to tell you: those who will just identify their identity into the oneness of each other, God shall serve them. God shall not only bless them—that's too little of a thing to ask for. God becomes the servant of those who amalgamate their egos and bring one identity out of the union of the two. They are such that God grants them the soul for which their generations will live forever. That is how saints are born on the earth.

"You can have children. Children can be born to you. You can have as many children as a whole football team. I have no problem with that. But a saint cannot be born to you, a master cannot be born to you, a divine human cannot be born to you if the amalgamation is not 'one.' Without that amalgamation of one, One cannot dwell. You can have a lot of sex, but you can never have that sixth sense, which can unite you beyond time and space. I can go on and on explaining it to you, but when I look at the whole thing, the loss is much more than the gain. The gain is much more than the loss if the amalgamation is real. And the amalgamation must succeed now and forever. That is the purpose of the institution of marriage, or even just living, or to be."

"What is an ideal marriage? It is a way of life in which a husband and wife compromise to face the time and space together for the security of their own life and their children."

> *Dhan pir e-eh naakheean behaan ikathe hoe.*[56]
> *Ek jot doe moortee, dhan pir kheeai soi.*
> "Don't call them together who sit together
> They are together who have one soul and two bodies."

"It must be a relationship of oneness. The happiness of marriage is based on the happiness of Infinity, not on condition. Whenever conditions come in the relationship of your life, life will become miserable, misery will engulf you, and happiness will run away, because happiness is nothing but Infinity. Happiness is not conditional, territorial, or personal. Happiness is Infinity. The moment you want to define it, you will kill the essence and create misery out of it.

Women in Training III: The Beaming Faculty of Woman" 1978

"Marriage is a carriage of happiness through the test of time."

YOGIC TECHNOLOGY TO THE RESCUE
THINGS TO DO

YOUR SPIRITUAL BANK ACCOUNT: SADHANA
"The family that prays together stays together." The Ladies Home Journal magazine ran that slogan in ads for an insurance company many years ago.

Whatever your spiritual path, the discipline of a consistent daily spiritual practice is the foundation of a complete marriage. In yogic terms, spiritual practice is called *sadhana*. It's the cement to hold together the bricks of the institution you are building together. You may be doing the 3HO *sadhana* or not, but for God's sake, before you start your day, before you face the outside world, do *something* to connect with your soul and the soul mate you have chosen!

Now comes the big challenge, brace yourself: The ideal time for *sadhana* is early in the morning, before sunrise. This is the time of day when meditation is most effective. It's very tempting, especially in the early months of marriage, when you're still dewy eyed and "honeymooning," to want to sleep in, and stay cozily nestled together under the quilts. But if you want the rest of your day, and the rest of your life to be excellent, you get up, get out, and do *sadhana* in what are called the *ambrosial* hours of the morning, 2-1/2 hours before sunrise, with a group of people when possible.

It's not easy getting up that early, but making the effort pays off. You're investing in your spiritual bank account, with a guaranteed 10% return on the time invested; you're covered for the next 24 hours!

If you don't already have a spiritual practice, let me tell you about the 3HO Sadhana that Yogi Bhajan taught. It starts with the recitation of *Japji Sahib*, whose syllables awaken the soul, followed by Kundalini Yoga exercises to tune up our body's 72,000 nerves, balance the glandular system and improve circulation. Working on overall health and well-being we get energized for the day. Next comes one hour of chanting mantras. These sound currents work on clearing out undesirable thoughts and feelings from the subconscious mind. The grand finale is to integrate everything by going to Gurdwara. After participating in sacred music and a prayer we hear the *hukam*. This is the "order of the day," a meditatively chosen "random" selection read from the Siri Guru Granth Sahib. It gives us something specific to meditate on, to contemplate, to integrate into our lives. If you understand the vibratory effect of sound, then you can understand how reciting or hearing divinely revealed words can elevate and purify your consciousness.

SHABD GURU

The Siri Guru Granth Sahib is a living Guru. This Shabd Guru is not a person, but a volume containing a compilation of Words spoken by enlightened men of various religions when they were in a state of Divine Union (yoga) with God. We tune in to that exalted vibratory frequency when we recite or listen to the Guru's Words. This experience is available to everyone and anyone, without restriction. You do not have to be a Sikh to avail yourself of its inspiration and guidance. Many yoga students go to Gurdwara to integrate and complete their morning *sadhana*.

By the way, any time you are having a problem in your life, in your marriage (most married people will encounter problems; it goes with the territory), an excellent way to restore perspective and get personal guidance from an impersonal, unbiased source is to go to the Siri Guru Granth Sahib. Sikh or not, Catholic, Protestant, Jew, Baptist, Muslim, Buddhist, or Jain, whatever religion you practice (or even if you don't), you can go to the universal Shabd Guru, offer a prayer, pose your question or problem, then meditatively "randomly" open the volume and read the first portion you see. This is your "hukam"—the order of the day. The Guru will speak to you—to your heart and soul.

AT THE END OF THE DAY...

In addition to morning sadhana, it's a smart idea for a couple to select a special meditation to do together every day. Evening is good time for this so you can each clear away the tensions and involvements of the day, and consciously strengthen your soul connection with each other.

WHY DO MANTRAS WORK?

You may wonder what good it is to chant syllables in a language that you might not understand. It's partly a matter of attunement, just as we tune the TV or the radio to whatever channel is broadcasting the program we want to receive. The mantras and meditations in this book are in the Gurmukhi language, which means "from the mouth of the Guru." Gurmukhi was derived from Sanskrit (the "Language of the Gods"), in which words come as close as possible to actually vibrating at the same frequency as the thing they describe.

Ancient yogis understood the technology of sound (*shabd*) and knew which combination of syllables would create what effect. It is a fact that whatever we attune ourselves to becomes a part of us. We are like magnets in a huge magnetic field, whatever we vibrate attracts "that" to us. Add to this the fact that the mantras were consciously designed knowing that as we chant aloud, our tongues stimulate some of the 84 pressure points on the soft upper palate in a specific sequence. This triggers a response from the hypothalamus gland, which in turn activates the pituitary. So an actual physiological change takes place in our brain chemistry.

As we vibrate, the Universe responds. Ever hear, "In the beginning was the Word, and the Word was with God"...? Everything in God's creation is vibrating. We just need to tune in to the wavelength that is broadcasting the program we want to experience. There are mantras we can use for almost any situation: to attract prosperity, give us courage, for self-healing or to call on God's power to heal others, to pray for a miracle—you name it, there's a mantra for it! And, of course, there is positive affirmation.

GRACE OF GOD MEDITATION FOR WOMEN

The technique of positive affirmation is nothing new. Words increase in power through repetition, and when you are repeating truth, the impact is profound. Combining the breath of life with words of power, Yogi Bhajan has given us one of the most effective affirmations a woman can use; it's called the "Grace of God Meditation."

The fact is, woman *is* the Grace of God. The problem is, she tends not to know it. The GGM meditation is designed to evoke and manifest the inner grace, coziness, strength, and radiance of each woman. It helps her to tune in directly with the *Adi Shakti*, the Primal Power, within her. It enables a woman to channel her emotions in a positive direction, strengthen her weaknesses, and develop mental clarity as well as to improve her physical and mental health.

All these claimed benefits don't mean a thing unless you do it. Yogi Bhajan taught us, "Doing is believing."

Try this meditation for 40 days. The best time to do it is at sunrise, and then again at sunset. (If you're going through menopause, doing it five times a day is recommended!) Be sure to do the GGM meditation on an empty stomach.

WOMEN, PART I

Lie down on your back, fully relaxing your face and body. Close your eyes. Breathing only through the nose, inhale deeply, hold the breath in while you silently repeat:

"*I am Grace of God*" ten times.

Exhale all the air out (through the nose), hold the breath out and silently repeat again:

"*I am Grace of God*" ten times.

Continue breathing and repeating the mantra in this manner for a total of five inhalations and five exhalations. This totals one hundred times that the affirmation is repeated mentally.

PART II

After the above cycle is completed, relax your breath, and with eyes still closed, slowly come sitting up into Easy Pose (cross legged). Bring your right hand into *gyan mudra* (index finger curled under the thumb, other three fingers stretched out straight, palm up, wrist resting on the knees, elbow straight). The left hand is held up next to the left shoulder, palm flat and facing forward (this is called the "vow position"), holding your hand as if you were taking an oath. Keep the breath relaxed and normal. Tense only one finger of the left hand at a time, keeping the other fingers straight but relaxed. Meditate on the governing energy of that finger *(see below)* while repeating aloud *five times, "I am Grace of God."*

Continue this sequence for the remaining fingers and the thumb, one at a time. Then if you wish, go back to any specific finger and concentrate on the particular characteristic it represents that you want to correct or enhance.

When both parts of the meditation are completed, lower the left hand and relax for a few minutes.

Your emotions will become more positively channeled and any physical or mental ill health will be greatly improved. Continue practicing for one year and your aura will become tipped with gold or silver; great strength and God's healing powers will flow through you.

WHAT CAN A MAN DO DURING THE GGM MEDITATION?

Men can sit up during the GGM meditation and silently affirm, *"I am in the Grace of God."* Yogi Bhajan has said that any country in which woman is not respected is doomed for destruction. He was adamant about restoring woman to her rightful place in society to fulfill her cosmic role, and in educating both men and women about their respective identities.

PLANETARY ENERGIES AT YOUR FINGER TIPS

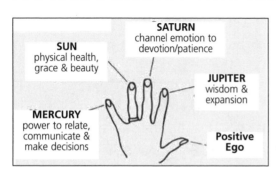

MERCURY (little finger): power to relate, communicate and make decisions

SUN/VENUS (ring finger): physical health, grace and beauty

SATURN (middle finger): channel emotion to devotion/patience

JUPITER (forefinger): wisdom and expansion

POSITIVE EGO: (thumb)

"Grace of God meditation will give you self-effectiveness." - Yogi Bhajan

YOGIC TIP

(A WORD TO THE WISE)

Consider this when you practice the following meditations. Yogi Bhajan gave the technical explanation for why yogis cover their heads to meditate. "Wearing a head covering enables you to command your sixth center, the *Agia* (*Ajna*) Chakra. Covering the head stabilizes the cerebral matter and the twenty-six parts of the brain, which are interlocked with the neurological system and electromagnetic field. This creates a focus of the functional circuit of the hemispheres, and tunes the neurological system. (The whole head is to be covered, not just the top of the head, using white natural fabric.)"[57]

You probably know that it is customary in many traditions to cover the head for worship or prayer. Just so, when chanting the *So Purkhs*, or *SA TA NA MA*, etc. which employ sacred syllables, it is a good idea to keep your head covered. Seen as a sign of reverence, now we know from a yogic perspective why it also makes the chanting more effective!

SO PURKH

THE MEDITATION FOR ALL WOMEN!

(from the Evening Prayer: Rehiras Sahib)

When you drop a pebble in a pond, the vibrations flow outward and affect everyone and everything they reach. Just so, when we chant sacred syllables, we are creating a sound current that sends out divine ripples. And, as we chant them, their inherent power becomes a part of our own vibration.

So Purkh is a divinely inspired combination of such syllables. It is Guru Ram Das' personal vision of God, yet its effect is not dependent upon any religion or belief system.

Yogi Bhajan spoke glowingly about the tremendous power and potential of reciting *So Purkh*'s. He said that a woman could use this shabd to beam on a man to:

- Attract a child to you who will become a man of God
- Heal a man
- Transform a man into a man of God
- Attract a man of God to be your husband
- Make God appear before you

Yogi Bhajan also said, "…You want to know about God? Read *So Purkh* in English. Find out all the faculties and then compare those faculties with you." He said it should be part of every woman's personal *sadhana*. "If you perfect it, you can talk to God person to person."

"It is a woman's special worship. The woman who will learn this *shabd* by heart and recite it will never have any difficulty as far as men are concerned. It is written that when a woman chants *So Purkh* 11 times a day before marriage, her husband shall turn out to be a God-like human being."

"The power of this *shabd* is that all bad faculties of the man you relate to are eliminated, and he becomes a divinely angelic person….Try it and just see what benefits and what beauty it brings to you."

Q: Do you have to recite it eleven times at once?

A: No. Eleven times in 24 hours.

Q: Is it effective silently?

A: …As a mantra you can do it silently, but when you do it as a sadhana, you do it as a sadhana. For extra goodies you have to do extra work. *(Ed. Note: I think he was saying that to get the maximum effect it really has to be done aloud.)*

Q: What if you want to sing it in the form of a *shabd*?

A: Oh, you should."[58]

Once upon a time, this really happened! A group of women went to Guru Ram Das begging him for help, saying, "You are the King, you are the Raj Yogi, you are sitting on the throne of Raj Yoga. Give us something which we may silently do so we can be free and liberated from the tyranny of the beasthood of the man."

He gave them *So Purkhs* to recite.

HOW TO CHANT IN NAAD YOGA

"Two lines form a *sutra* (couplet)—that means a whole breath length should be used and completed. And it should be smooth. Don't inhale in between. In the breath is a total smoothness. Do one *sutra* per breath and then your rhythm will be complete. If you breathe in between then it will disturb the rhythm and the *sutra* will not be complete; that is called the basic recitation in the Naad Yoga."   Yogi Bhajan

SO PURKH: GURMUKHI · TRANSLITERATION · TRANSLATION
English translation by MSS Guruka Singh Khalsa

ਰਾਗ ਆਸਾ ਮਹਲਾ ਚੌਥਾ ਸੋ ਪੁਰਖ

Raag[59] Aasaa Guru Ram Das Sopurkh[60]

ੴ ਸਤਿਗੁਰ ਪ੍ਰਸਾਦਿ ॥

ik-ongkaar satgur parsaad

I Know that I am One with God. This is my True Guru's Gift

ਸੋ ਪੁਰਖੁ ਨਿਰੰਜਨ ਹਰਿ ਪੁਰਖੁ ਨਿਰੰਜਨ ਹਰਿ ਅਗਮਾ ਅਗਮ ਅਪਾਰਾ ॥

so purakh niranjan har purakh niranjan har agmaa agam apaaraa.

The Primal One is perfectly pure. The Primal God is perfect. He is within all and beyond all.

ਸਭਿ ਧਿਆਵਹਿ ਸਭਿ ਧਿਆਵਹਿ ਤੁਧੁ ਜੀ ਹਰਿ ਸਚੇ ਸਿਰਜਨਹਾਰਾ ॥

sabh dhi-aavahi sabh dhi-aavahi tudh jee har sachay sirjanhaaraa.

Everyone meditates. All souls meditate on You, O True Creator.

ਸਭਿ ਜੀਅ ਤੁਮਾਰੇ ਜੀ ਤੂੰ ਜੀਆ ਕਾ ਦਾਤਾਰਾ ॥

sabh jee-a tumaaray jee too(n) jee-aa kaa daataaraa.

All souls are one with You. All souls come from You.

ਹਰਿ ਧਿਆਵਹੁ ਸੰਤਹੁ ਜੀ ਸਭਿ ਦੂਖ ਵਿਸਾਰਣਹਾਰਾ ॥

har dhi-aavahu santahu jee sabh dookh visaaranhaaraa.

O Saints, meditate on God and all pains will fly away.

ਹਰਿ ਆਪੇ ਠਾਕੁਰੁ ਹਰਿ ਆਪੇ ਸੇਵਕੁ ਜੀ ਕਿਆ ਨਾਨਕ ਜੰਤ ਵਿਚਾਰਾ ॥੧॥

har aapay thaakur har aapay sayvak jee ki-aa naanak jant vichaaraa. ॥1॥

God Himself is the Master. God Himself is the Servant.

O Nanak, everyone is empty-handed before Him.

ਤੂੰ ਘਟ ਘਟ ਅੰਤਰਿ ਸਰਬ ਨਿਰੰਤਰਿ ਜੀ ਹਰਿ ਏਕੋ ਪੁਰਖੁ ਸਮਾਣਾ ॥

too(n) ghat ghat antar sarab nirantar jee har ayko purakh samaanaa.

You are in each beat of my heart, and in all hearts. O Lord, you are the One in everyone.

ਇਕਿ ਦਾਤੇ ਇਕਿ ਭੇਖਾਰੀ ਜੀ ਸਭਿ ਤੇਰੇ ਚੋਜ ਵਿਡਾਣਾ ॥

ik daatay ik bhaykhaaree jee sabh tayray choj vidaanaa.

Some are givers and some are takers. This is all Your play.

ਤੂੰ ਆਪੇ ਦਾਤਾ ਆਪੇ ਭੁਗਤਾ ਜੀ ਹਉ ਤੁਧੁ ਬਿਨੁ ਅਵਰੁ ਨ ਜਾਣਾ ॥

too(n) aapay daataa aapay bhugtaa jee ha-o tudh bin avar na jaanaa.

You are the Giver and You are the receiver. It is all You.

ਤੂੰ ਪਾਰਬ੍ਰਹਮੁ ਬੇਅੰਤੁ ਬੇਅੰਤੁ ਜੀ ਤੇਰੇ ਕਿਆ ਗੁਣ ਆਖਿ ਵਖਾਣਾ ॥

too(n) paarbrahm bay-ant bay-ant jee tayray ki-aa gun aakh vakhaanaa.

You are the God of all; endless and Infinite. I have no words to describe your virtues.

ਜੋ ਸੇਵਹਿ ਜੋ ਸੇਵਹਿ ਤੁਧੁ ਜੀ ਜਨੁ ਨਾਨਕੁ ਤਿਨ ਕੁਰਬਾਣਾ ॥੨॥

jo sayveh jo sayveh tudh jee jan naanak tin kurbaanaa. ॥2॥

O Lord, Nanak is a sacrifice unto those who serve and serve You forever. ॥2॥

ਹਰਿ ਧਿਆਵਹਿ ਹਰਿ ਧਿਆਵਹਿ ਤੁਧੁ ਜੀ ਸੇ ਜਨ ਜੁਗ ਮਹਿ ਸੁਖਵਾਸੀ ॥

har dhi-aavahi har dhi-aavahi tudh jee say jan jug meh sukhvaasee.

Meditate on God. Meditate on God and your soul will be at peace in this world.

ਸੇ ਮੁਕਤੁ ਸੇ ਮੁਕਤੁ ਭਏ ਜਿਨ ਹਰਿ ਧਿਆਇਆ ਜੀ ਤਿਨ ਤੂਟੀ ਜਮ ਕੀ ਫਾਸੀ ॥

say mukat say mukat bha-ay jin har dhi-aa-i-aa jee tin tootee jam kee faasee.

Meditate on God and live free. Live free and know the noose of death is meaningless.

ਜਿਨ ਨਿਰਭਉ ਜਿਨ ਹਰਿ ਨਿਰਭਉ ਧਿਆਇਆ ਜੀ ਤਿਨ ਕਾ ਭਉ ਸਭੁ ਗਵਾਸੀ ॥
jin nirbha-o jin har nirbha-o dhi-aa-i-aa jee tin kaa bha-o sabh gavaasee.
Meditate on the fearless One, the fearless God, and live free from fear.

ਜਿਨ ਸੇਵਿਆ ਜਿਨ ਸੇਵਿਆ ਮੇਰਾ ਹਰਿ ਜੀ ਤੇ ਹਰਿ ਹਰਿ ਰੂਪਿ ਸਮਾਸੀ ॥
jin sayvi-aa jin sayvi-aa mayraa har jee tay har har roop samaasee.
Those who serve, O those who serve my Lord, are one with Har and they look divine.

ਸੇ ਧੰਨੁ ਸੇ ਧੰਨੁ ਜਿਨ ਹਰਿ ਧਿਆਇਆ ਜੀ ਜਨੁ ਨਾਨਕੁ ਤਿਨ ਬਲਿ ਜਾਸੀ ॥3॥
say dhan say dhan jin har dhi-aa-i-aa jee jan naanak tin bal jaasee. ||3||
Blessed, O blessed are they who meditate on Har. Servant Nanak is a sacrifice to them. ||3||

ਤੇਰੀ ਭਗਤਿ ਤੇਰੀ ਭਗਤਿ ਭੰਡਾਰ ਜੀ ਭਰੇ ਬਿਅੰਤ ਬੇਅੰਤਾ ॥
tayree bhagat tayree bhagat bhandaar jee bharay bi-ant bay-antaa.
Devotion to You, O devotion to You is a treasure trove that ever overflows.

ਤੇਰੇ ਭਗਤ ਤੇਰੇ ਭਗਤ ਸਲਾਹਨਿ ਤੁਧੁ ਜੀ ਹਰਿ ਅਨਿਕ ਅਨੇਕ ਅਨੰਤਾ ॥
tayray bhagat tayray bhagat salaahan tudh jee har anik anayk anantaa.
Your lovers, O Your lovers praise You, my Beloved, forever and ever.

ਤੇਰੀ ਅਨਿਕ ਤੇਰੀ ਅਨਿਕ ਕਰਹਿ ਹਰਿ ਪੂਜਾ ਜੀ ਤਪੁ ਤਾਪਹਿ ਜਪਹਿ ਬੇਅੰਤਾ ॥
tayree anik tayree anik karahi har poojaa jee tap taapeh jaapeh bay-antaa.
For You, just for You O Lord, so many poojas are performed and so many
endlessly chant and discipline themselves.

ਤੇਰੇ ਅਨੇਕ ਤੇਰੇ ਅਨੇਕ ਪੜਹਿ ਬਹੁ ਸਿਮ੍ਰਿਤਿ ਸਾਸਤ ਜੀ ਕਰਿ ਕਿਰਿਆ ਖਟੁ ਕਰਮ ਕਰੰਤਾ
tayray anayk tayray anayk parheh baho simrit saasat jee kar kiri-aa khat karam karantaa.
For You, just for You O Lord, so many read the Smirtis and Shastras.
They do *kriyas* and ceremonies.

ਸੇ ਭਗਤ ਸੇ ਭਗਤ ਭਲੇ ਜਨ ਨਾਨਕ ਜੀ ਜੋ ਭਾਵਹਿ ਮੇਰੇ ਹਰਿ ਭਗਵੰਤਾ ॥੪॥

say bhagat say bhagat bhalay jan naanak jee jo bhaaveh mayray har bhagvantaa. ||4||

Those lovers, those lovers are sublime, O servant Nanak, who are pleasing to God.

ਤੂੰ ਆਦਿ ਪੁਰਖੁ ਅਪਰੰਪਰੁ ਕਰਤਾ ਜੀ ਤੁਧੁ ਜੇਵਡੁ ਅਵਰੁ ਨ ਕੋਈ ॥

too(n) aad purakh aprampar kartaa jee tudh jayvad avar na ko-ee.

You are the Primal One, the most awesome Creator of everything.
There is none as great as You.

ਤੂੰ ਜੁਗੁ ਜੁਗੁ ਏਕੋ ਸਦਾ ਸਦਾ ਤੂੰ ਏਕੋ ਜੀ ਤੂੰ ਨਿਹਚਲੁ ਕਰਤਾ ਸੋਈ ॥

too(n) jug jug ayko sadaa sadaa too(n) ayko jee too(n) nihachal kartaa so-ee.

Throughout time and beyond time, You are the One, constant and True Creator.

ਤੁਧੁ ਆਪੇ ਭਾਵੈ ਸੋਈ ਵਰਤੈ ਜੀ ਤੂੰ ਆਪੇ ਕਰਹਿ ਸੁ ਹੋਈ ॥

tudh aapay bhaavai so-ee vartai jee too(n) aapay karahi so ho-ee.

You do everything, and everything happens according to Your Will.

ਤੁਧੁ ਆਪੇ ਸ੍ਰਿਸਟਿ ਸਭ ਉਪਾਈ ਜੀ ਤੁਧੁ ਆਪੇ ਸਿਰਜਿ ਸਭ ਗੋਈ ॥

tudh aapay sarisat sabh upaa-ee jee tudh aapay siraj sabh go-ee.

You create the whole universe. You destroy it and create it again.

ਜਨੁ ਨਾਨਕੁ ਗੁਣ ਗਾਵੈ ਕਰਤੇ ਕੇ ਜੀ ਜੋ ਸਭਸੈ ਕਾ ਜਾਣੋਈ ॥੫॥੧॥

jan naanak gun gaavai kartay kay jee jo sabhsai kaa jaano-ee. ||5||1||

Servant Nanak sings the praises of his beloved Lord forever and ever.
He is the Knower within all souls. ||5||1||

MANTRA FOR A MIRACLE
DHAN DHAN RAAM DAAS GUR

When you need a Miracle, this mantra in praise of Guru Ram Das is the one to chant.

DHAN DHAN RAAM DAAS GUR   HAIL HAIL GURU RAM DAS JI

Dhan Dhan Raam Daas Gur
Jin siri-aa tinai savaari-aa

Honored and Praised is Ram Das the Guru.
The Lord, who created You, He alone has embellished You.

Pooree ho-ee karaamaat
Aap sirajanahaarai dhaari-aa

Perfect is Your Miracle:
The Creator Himself has installed You on the Throne.

Sikhee atai sangatee
Paarbrahm kar naamasakaari-aa

Your Sikhs, and the entire congregation, bow and revere
You as the Supreme Lord.

Atal athaaho atoll too
Tayraa ant na paaravaari-aa

You are Unshakable, Unfathomable, and Immeasurable.
Your extent is beyond limit.

Jinee too(n) sayvi-aa bhaa-o kar
Say tudh paar ootaari-aa

They who serve You with love, are carried across the
world-ocean by You.

Labh lobh kaam krodh moho
Maar kadhay tudh saparvaari-aa

Greed, attachment, lust, anger, and ego—these five
passions have been beaten and driven out by You.

Dhan so tayraa thaan hai
Sach tayraa paiskaari-aa

Honored is Your Place,
True are Your Bounties.

Naanak too Lehnaa too hai
Gur Amar too veechaari-aa
Gur dithaa taa(n) man saadhaari-aa

You are Nanak, You are Angad, and You are
Guru Amar Das—so do I recognize You.
Seeing the Guru, my soul is sustained.

SODARSHAN CHAKRA KRIYA

As taught by Yogi Bhajan, Master of Kundalini Yoga

"Of all the 20 types of yoga, including Kundalini Yoga, this is the highest *kriya*. This meditation cuts through all darkness. It will give you a new start. It is the simplest *kriya*, but at the same time the hardest. It cuts through all barriers of the neurotic or psychotic inside-nature. When a person is in a very bad state, techniques imposed from the outside will not work. The pressure has to be stimulated from within.

"Tragedy of life is when the subconscious releases garbage into the conscious mind. This *kriya* invokes the Kundalini to give you the necessary vitality and intuition to combat the negative effects of the subconscious mind."

POSITION: Sit with a straight spine.

EYES: Gazing at the tip of the nose.

BREATH: Block off the right nostril with the right thumb. Inhale slowly and deeply through the left nostril. Hold the breath while you mentally chant *Wahe Guru (wha-hay guroo)* 16 times, pumping the navel point 3 times with each repetition (pump once on *Wha*, once on *Hay*, and once on *Guru*—for a total of 48 pumps).

b. Release the right nostril. Place the right index finger (pinkie finger can also be used) to block off the left nostril. Exhale slowly and completely through the right nostril.

Repeat the sequence (a and b).

TO END: Inhale, hold 5-10 seconds, then exhale. (Breathe only through the nose.) Then stretch and shake every part of your body for about 1 minute to circulate the energy.

TIME CONSTRAINTS: There is no time, no place, no space and no condition attached to this *kriya*. Each garbage pit has its own time to clear. If you are going to clean your own garbage, you must estimate and clean it as fast as you can, or as slow as you want. You have to decide how much time you have to clean up your garbage pit.

You may start with just a few minutes and gradually increase the time. Some suggested lengths for practice of *Sodarshan Chakra Kriya* are 31 or 62 minutes a day.

YOGIC TRADITION TELLS US: If you can do this meditation for 62 minutes to start with, and develop to the point that you can do it 2-1/2 hours a day (1/10th of the day), it will give you the following: *Nao niddhi, athara siddhi* (nine precious virtues and 18 occult powers). And in those 27 total virtues of the world lies the entire universe. So start with 31 minutes, then after a while, do it for 40 minutes, then for 62 minutes. Take time to graduate in it.

When practiced 2-1/2 hours every day, it makes a "perfect superman" out of you. It purifies, it takes care of the human life, and brings together all 27 facets of life and makes a human perfect, saintly, successful, and qualified.

"This meditation also gives one the pranic power. This *kriya* never fails. It can give one all the inner happiness, and bring one to a state of ecstasy in life."

SAT KRIYA

This is a very powerful *kriya*, a complete action in itself. Yogi Bhajan reminds us, *SAT NAM* is the *bij* or "seed" mantra. It is small and potent. Great things grow from it. If it is not written in your destiny to be with God and know higher consciousness, this mantra engraves it in your destiny. Sat Kriya purifies your being... all improper things will leave you."

The following are general instructions. When you are doing it with your partner, you sit back to back, with spines touching.

▸ Sit in Easy Pose (crossed legged), or in Rock Pose (on your heels under your sitting bones, knees together), or in Full Lotus.

▸ Raise your arms up over your head with elbows straight, with the upper arms hugging the sides of the head.

▸ Interlock your fingers, leaving the index fingers pointing straight up. Keep your chest lifted and your shoulder blades down. Maintain the neck lock (chin is pulled straight back).

▸ Keep your arms straight. Close your eyes and focus at the Third Eye Point (the root of the nose, between your eyebrows—and up about 1/8 inch), the Sixth Chakra.

▸ Begin to chant *SAT NAAM* with a constant rhythm of about 8 times per 10 seconds.

As you chant *SAT* (rhymes with "but") "suck" in the sound, powerfully pulling the navel in and up toward the spine.

With the sound *NAAM* (rhymes with "baa"—and is very quiet), relax and release the belly.

The focus of the sound *NAAM* can be either at the Navel Point or at the Brow Point.

‣ The Breath regulates itself.

‣ There is an automatic simultaneous contraction of the rectum and sex organ areas (as in the *Mulbandh*, the lower body lock, but the lock is pulled from the navel) each time you chant *SAT*.

‣ To finish, inhale and hold the breath for 5-10 seconds as you pull strongly in and up on your navel, drawing your energy up from the base of your spine to the top of your head. Breathing only through your nose, exhale and repeat that sequence one more time. On the third breath, inhale, exhale completely, and hold the breath out for 5-10 seconds as you apply all the locks[61] (neck lock, diaphragm lock, root lock) while you feel the energy rising up your spine.

If this is your first experience with Sat Kriya, start with just one minute! Then, after practicing it for a few days, go to 2 minutes, then increase to 3 minutes and gradually (add a minute each day) work up to 11 minutes. When you feel ready, you can gradually work up to 31 minutes. However long you practice this *kriya*, relax afterwards for at least the same amount of time.

SITALEE PRANAYAM[62]

Yogic breathing techniques are called *Pranayam*. *Sitalee Pranayam* is known to have a powerful cooling, relaxing effect on the body, while maintaining alertness. It is known to lower fevers, and aid digestion. How to do it:

‣ Extend your tongue out beyond the lips and curl it into a "U" shape.

‣ Inhale deeply through the curled tongue.

‣ Exhale completely through the nose.

Continue for at least 2 or 3 minutes (or 26 times in the morning and 26 times in the evening[63]). You may notice a bitter taste at first. This is a sign of detoxificatiin and will pass.

KIRTAN KRIYA (Habit re-forming!)
31-MINUTE MEDITATION

This meditation is especially useful when you want to get rid of habits that are counter-productive to your happiness. Instead of trying to "break" bad habits (which doesn't work, because the more attention you give to anything, the stronger it gets), the approach is to substitute a positive habit for the negative one.

The practice of *Kirtan Kriya* works positively, empowering you to change your behavior patterns. This combination of syllables is a powerful catalyst for change.

Sit with your spine straight. Eyes are closed. With your hands resting on your knees, press the tip of the thumb of each hand firmly to each of the fingertips of that hand in sequence, starting with the forefingers, while chanting each syllable in turn. Be sure as you chant each syllable to press firmly enough so that when you release the pressure, the tip of the finger is briefly white. If you press too gently you'll put yourself to sleep!

The syllables are:

SA	Totality (All that ever was, is, or shall be)
TA	Creativity (The principle of Creation)
NA	Destruction (Crucifixion)
MA	Regeneration (Resurrection)

Keep moving your fingers through the entire meditation.

SA	press the thumb and forefinger (A)
TA	press the thumb and middle finger (B)
NA	press the thumb and ring finger (C)
MA	press the thumb and little finger (D)

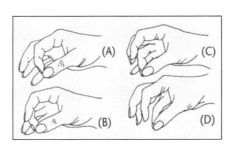

- First five minutes chant ALOUD
- Next five minutes chant in a LOUD WHISPER
- Ten minutes chant SILENTLY
- Five minutes LOUD WHISPER
- Five minutes ALOUD

Inhale deeply, lift your arms straight up in the air and vigorously shake out the fingers for approximately one minute. Relax.

AJAI ALAI MANTRA

Ajai Alai is from *Jaap Sahib*, the powerful epic poem praising God. Its power is to give you, among other things, extreme intuitive awareness. Yogi Bhajan said it was best to listen[64] to it and try to copy the sounds you hear, rather than just recite from the printed words. (But here's the transliteration anyway.)

Ajai, Alai, Abhai, Abai,
Abhoo, Ajoo, Anaas, Akaas
Agunj, Abunj, Alukh, Abukh,
Akaal, Dayaal, Alaykh, Abhaykh
Anaam, Akaam, Aghaahaa, Adhaahaa,
Anaatay, Paramaatay, Ajonee, Amonee,
Na Raagay, Na Rangay, Na Roopay, Na Raykay,
Akaramang, Abharamang, Aganjay, Alaykhay.

Invincible, Indestructible, Fearless, Unchanging,
Unformed, Unborn, Imperishable, Etheric,
Unbreakable, Impenetrable, Unseen, Unaffected,
Undying, Merciful, Indescribable, Incorruptible.
Nameless, Desireless, Unfathomable, Incorruptible.
Unmastered, Destroyer, Beyond birth, Beyond silence.
Beyond love, Beyond color, Beyond form, Beyond shape.
Beyond karma, Beyond doubt, Unconquerable, Indescribable.

EK ONG KAR SAT GUR PRASAD
SAT GUR PRASAD EK ONG KAR

Mantra to change negativity to positivity.

THE PERSIAN WHEEL (GATGA)

When your smile disappears and you wear a frown
It shows your thinking's upside down.

Better look at your mind and see what's in it—
then with this mantra, you can fix it in a minute!

Whatever the worry that's pulling you down
You can use this sound to turn it around:

EK ONG KAAR SAT GUR PRASAAD
SAT GUR PRASAAD EK ONG KAAR

It's quite simple, why not try it,
Give it a whirl, I think you'll buy it!

Repeat five times, it will change your mood
from negative to positive—
From rotten—feel good!

Like the tiny stick on the Persian wheel
That works to reverse the spin
This mantra controls the mind
No matter what state you're in

Change your direction and you will see
From mind's domination you'll be free.

METHODS FOR MEN

ARCHER POSE

Chivalry and fearlessness, inherent in this noble warrior stance,
Physical stamina and strength in feet, thighs and arms enhanced.
Archer also puts pressure on the thigh bone,
Balancing calcium, magnesium, potassium, and sodium.

On the physical plane, we have lots of reasons for doing Archer Pose. It helps develop strength in the quadriceps and the intestines. The legs and knees are being strengthened. Outstanding physical stamina and strength are gained, while, remarkably, at the same time, there is an inner posture of feelings taking place that is equal in power to the pure physical connection of feet to the ground. Sometimes called the "Hero" posture, Archer Pose develops Courage. That is its special inner gift. Plus, it is said that the need for excessive sleep disappears!

FROG POSE (MANDAKASANA)

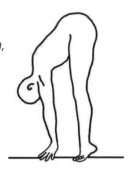

Protruding belly? Short of breath? Want to jump and hop?
Frog Pose unifies prana and apana
Slowly build up to twenty-six repetitions, then stop!
Squatting keeping heels "glued" together, rise up and down on the toes.

Inhale, straighten your legs as your hips go up and your head goes down,
Fingertips, placed between the knees, stay firmly on the ground.
Alternate from squatting to straight as Frog Pose you apply,
Transforming and elevating sex energy from lower chakras to high.
Whether you do them slow, or do them fast
Frogs solve stomach ailments and eliminate gas.

CHAPTER TWELVE

UP CLOSE & PERSONAL
REAL STORIES

THE GRACE OF THE WRECKING BALL
BY SIRI VED KAUR KHALSA · LOS ANGELES, CA

I promised Shakti I would write a few paragraphs about the first year of marriage; how the expectations and ideals we have before marriage don't necessarily have anything to do with the real world. But here I am, married for nearly 18 years, and most of the issues I wanted to address are just as present now as they were back in 1987, simply with different, deeper layers.

Perhaps what happens early on in marriage is the realization that all is not going according to our plans. If we are lucky, we recognize that there is another, greater plan underlying all things. This plan provides unexpected challenges and unpleasant discoveries. It sometimes seems like a wrecking ball, the way it can swing back and forth and completely wipe out our plans. Its purpose is not to make life and marriage smooth and blissful. The purpose of this "Greater Plan" is to encourage us to grow spiritually, emotionally, and in relation to one another, and through this find our own bliss.

This has been my experience anyway, and it is now my privilege to share a few of the lessons I have learned by the grace of the wrecking ball.

UNTIL I WAS MARRIED TO GURUJODHA SINGH, the last thing I ever would have called myself was a manipulative woman. Simply not me! I was completely unaware of the ways I manipulated men sexually, socially, and emotionally. My husband, bless his heart, simply did not respond to my wiles and this freaked me out to the point I was certain he did not love me. He apparently has an innate radar for neediness and

for the slightest effort on my part to change him in any way. He'd sense it and simply not give me any energy back. He wouldn't engage in my game, a game that I was completely unaware of playing. So, I had to learn to communicate honestly and without a hidden agenda (however, I do find that some hidden agendas, those built of pure and nurturing intent, fare well; anything else is simply counter-productive and a waste of energy). I am still learning.

Once I realized that I could not make my husband change, I was miserable. Once I realized that I did not particularly desire to live the rest of my life in misery, I recognized that completely accepting my husband was the only way to go. This means accepting and loving the whole entire package of who he is in every aspect. "What? You mean that I have to accept and love the fact that my husband Joe is_____?!" (Readers: insert your own pet peeve) you might ask. Well, sort of. The key is to focus on the strengths and qualities that we admire and that inspire us. Learn from nature: The plant that is watered grows. As for the areas in which your spouse could be perceived as weak…don't give any energy to that perception. Remember, it's your perception. He doesn't see it the same way.

However, some things simply cannot be ignored. These things must be talked about, and that's the third thing I would like to share. You must talk and share your Selves. This works best for Gurujodha and me late at night. We just lie in bed and talk and talk and talk. Spiritual talk. Household talk. Dirty laundry talk. Taxes talk. Dreams talk. Difficult talk. Anything talk. Heart to heart talking also ranks way high in terms of foreplay, in case you didn't know. So much so, that our code word for sex is "discussion." For instance, I might send him an email that says something like, "Honey, have you heard about such and such? Let's discuss it tonight." He knows exactly what I mean and will be thinking about it all day until we hit the sheets. (This kind of manipulation, based on pure and nurturing intention, as mentioned above, is absolutely fine by the way.)

The last thing I'll mention, and for many people this is the most difficult, is to avoid measuring and counting everything. Remember that relationships, like life, are not necessarily "fair." I have given up on counting how many more hours I spend doing housework than my husband. I am fairly certain he does not keep track of all the things I do that must annoy him. Getting along requires compromise and, sometimes, sacrifice. Sometimes it hurts. Sometimes it's liberating. And if you deeply feel there is an issue that simply will not tolerate compromise, you must honestly talk about it.

Then, of course, discuss it.

MANTRA FOR MIRACLES
GURU MEHER KAUR KHALSA · ESPANOLA, NM

IN 1978 I TRAVELED TO INDIA on a wonderful 40 day yatra (spiritual journey). Afterwards, I realized that for the first time in my life I was in a deep depression. My emotions were touchy and I felt like crying all the time, even though I was surrounded by family, friends, and the busy life in the Miami Ashram. Those concerned called my Teacher, the Siri Singh Sahib (Yogi Bhajan), and I tearfully tried to explain the unexplainable, saying, "I'm so depressed." His reply in no uncertain terms was "Don't be!" Well, that was that, and I felt 100% lighter and brighter. He said he would see me soon on his annual Miami visit.

The sadness in my heart originated from my concern about the unhealthy, negative lifestyles my two sons had chosen. I had already accepted the fact that my husband of over 30 years still held to his old habits of smoking, and sometimes drinking. I found it easy to overlook his vices and decidedly rough exterior, because of all his wonderful, endearing qualities.

We had comfortably adjusted to the fact I was a Sikh and he was not. As long as I soft-pedaled my love and devotion to my Teacher, who, after all, was my age and younger than my husband, all went surprisingly smoothly. Busily the Ashram prepared for the arrival of the Siri Singh Sahib. As usual, my husband planned to be away—"giving us more room."

When I had an audience with my Teacher he compassionately listened and then told me to keep the *Shabd*, *Dhan Dhan Ram Das Guru*, going in my head all the time. As a Gemini there is always something going on in my head, so I was delighted to follow his directions. I knew this was going to manifest everything I wanted to happen! This was the *"Shabd* for miracles!"

Quite some time later, with a laugh, I realized the real miracle was the change in me! The weight of the world had lifted and was replaced by profound inner happiness. Why had I ever felt anything was "wrong"?

Then one spring afternoon, out of the blue, my husband asked for an audience with the Siri Singh Sahib who once again was visiting us in Miami. The room was full of the Florida sangat (spiritual community). The Siri Singh Sahib pierced my husband with his eyes saying, "Well, what do you want?"

"I want to come home, Sir." Yogiji roared with laughter! Everyone cheered and laughed while I was struck dumb! From that day on Robert Guest became Guru Meher Singh Khalsa, Sikh of the Guru. The miracle of Guru Ram Das gave us ten wonderful years of sharing completely our love of God, Guru, Teacher and Sangat.

On Sept 25, 1994, my husband of 47 years was nearing the end of his life's journey. The Siri Singh Sahib called the hospital room saying, "All karmas are paid." When my husband heard, he closed his eyes and said, "I think I'll go now." With the soft chanting of *Wahe Guru*, his cherished family said goodbye. Later I received a dear letter from the Siri Singh Sahib, which ended with these words:

"Teach others to understand the depth, power, and grace of a commitment that lasts even beyond Death."

The lives of my sons didn't change in the sense I had expected. They matured, married, and became fathers (now one is a grandfather!) with the usual ups-and-downs of life. One son and his family are vegetarians, both sons have kept their beards and uncut hair. Neither smoke anymore and there are no drugs and very little alcohol involved. When I changed and relaxed about what I thought should happen, gracefully things did smooth out in my sons' lives. But the thing I never dreamed would happen, was the miracle that happened in my husband's life, and therefore in mine!

Wahe Guru Ji ka Khalsa, Wahe Guru Ji ki Fateh![65]

THE POWER OF PRAYER

BY RA-EL CORSINI AKA SARB NAM KAUR

Owner and Artistic Director of The Flying Lotus Movement Center, Mt. Shasta, California

MY PERSONAL VOYAGE WITH THE SIRI SINGH SAHIB (Yogi Bhajan) began in 1992, at The Whole Life Expo in Los Angeles, California. I was a volunteer who kept "time" for each of the celebrated presenters, and I got to pick and choose which workshop I wanted to experience. I knew nothing of the Sikhs or of Yogi Bhajan, but my heart drew me to his teachings that day.

My life in Los Angeles was a wild ride of modeling, acting, dancing, waitressing, and partying. I received a taste of Yogiji's brilliance, but wasn't ready to take the bite. It wasn't till years later when my mother began taking weekly classes and went into the Teacher Training program with Deva Kaur in Florida, that my ears perked up to hear the teachings of Yogi Bhajan once again. By this time, I had chosen to be in an emotionally abusive relationship with a boyfriend in Colorado for five years.

My mother invited my daughter and me to go to Women's Camp in Espanola, NM. I was delighted! At that point in my relationship, I would take any opportunity to be away, because I had fallen into a pattern and was deeply in fear of changing it. The year I went to Women's Camp, every day had a different theme: Grace, Courage, Strength, and more. I learned powerful mantras, mudras, yoga sets and breath techniques that awakened every cell in my body. On the day with the theme Courage, we rappelled down a cliff. I had never even considered doing anything like that in this life! As I raised the courage within myself to go down, I recognized that you had to put your body in an "L" shape to reach the bottom successfully and with ease. I imagined the hands of God beneath me, and as I trusted and chanted *Ek Ong Kar Sat Guru Prasaad Sat Guru Prasaad Ek Ong Kar* (to flip my mind into the positive), I freely made it down!

Nightly we sang *Ajai Alai*[66] with Yogi Bhajan and tears flowed from my soul as I felt blissful transformation. I knew in my heart I had gained the courage to face my partner at home and no longer would allow the unhealthy patterns to continue. I returned home in full *bana,*[67] holding my grace, carrying my strength and courage in raw empowerment.

As my partner argued and spewed out hurtful words, I silently chanted *Ek Ong Kar Sat Guru Prasaad Sat Guru Prasaad Ek Ong Kar* until he backed off, repelled by my energy field of light, strength and protection.

I left the relationship and became a single mother again. Chanting *Har Haray Haree* every day brought everything I needed to thrive and chanting *Ajai Alai* mantra every day for a year, manifested a relationship of honor, trust, grace and upliftment. My beloved husband has been a glorious rebirth for my daughter and my spirits. We live in magical Mt. Shasta, California, fulfilling our dreams daily.

Every 40 days I choose a mantra to commit to…and witness the miracles.

(Editor's Note: The mantras she mentions are available on CD. See Sources and Resources. Also, in the interests of "truth in advertising" the more recent Women's Camps have not featured rappelling!)

THE FANTASY OF THE OTHER WOMAN
(AUTHOR WISHED TO REMAIN ANONYMOUS)

MY HUSBAND AND I WERE IN OUR EARLY THIRTIES and married for 12 years, when he was attracted to one of his clients, and she to him. I did not know the specific details of the situation at the time, but I felt a difference in our relationship, as if it was on shaky ground. I immediately started doing the "marriage-saver" meditation taught to me by Yogi Bhajan. It included doing eleven repetitions of *So Purkh*[68] a day, and visualizing my husband as pure, virtuous, and manifesting his highest potential.

A few weeks later, my spouse (on his own) consulted with our teacher, Yogi Bhajan, who was in town for meetings. They discussed how "following" this attraction would be a dead end, benefiting no one. Yogi Bhajan gave my husband an exercise that he said would end the attraction. He said, "Go through the fantasy to the end and then say *Wahe Guru* out loud, and keep doing it until there are no more fantasies." My husband responded, "Sir, I don't think you understand how strong this is. I need something really powerful to get rid of this." Yogi Bhajan smiled and said, "Just try it, and do it now. Then come back and tell me how it worked."

One half hour later, the attraction was 90% gone. In just 30 short minutes, my husband felt free from the mirage that had been haunting him. He never acted on the attraction, and our relationship has continued to deepen in trust, respect and mutual understanding for over thirty years of marriage.

We carry on using the practical, yet sacred technology taught by Yogi Bhajan to make our lives healthy, happy, and whole. We are ever grateful to him and for the blessing that we can, in turn, share this effective technology with others.

SHAKTI'S FAMOUS TALK REMEMBERED
BY SAT JIVAN KAUR KHALSA · NEW YORK CITY

Sat Nam Dearest Shakti Parwha Kaur Ji,

It took me awhile to go back so far in the old memory banks but I do recall the time I heard your "Don't Get Married" talk. It was at the June, 1971, Summer Solstice, in Paonia, Colorado. If memory serves me, you spoke to the ladies interested in getting married, out in the yard area under a tree. I'm pretty sure you had a sari on, is that right? You read the *Lavan*[69] from the *Peace Lagoon* to us as part of the wedding ceremony.

Shakti Ji, if I recall, this was your famous talk, deeply explaining commitment, the Sikh view of marriage, our options for going forward, and the non-judgmental option that "maybe now was not the right time to get married." I remember feeling challenged and yet reassured that this was exactly what I was looking for in marriage, and that this was the kind of commitment I wanted in marriage. I also made a clear commitment to myself that I didn't have to get it all perfect instantly, I just needed to keep trying, without ever quitting. In other words I had the rest of my life to get it right.

So here I am 34 years later, just thinking this morning that I only have 16 more years until Sat Jivan Singh and I will be married for 50 years! We are both fond of telling people that we have thought of murder often, but divorce never!

Thank you for giving me the gift of your famous talk, I am grateful. I look forward to seeing your book.

All love in Divine,
Sat Jivan Kaur

ELSA'S TRUE STORY
BY ELSA FOX · FLORIDA

I AM MARRIED TO A WONDERFUL DOCTOR with a big heart, who helps many people. The challenge I faced was that he was always moody when he arrived home from the office. It felt like he was pushing me and the children away. His language was angry and disrespectful towards us. Nothing I did or said seemed to affect the situation. I actually felt like there was fire coming from his mouth.

I was completely desperate, and crying. I told my yoga teacher, "I just don't know what to do with this man. I know he has potential; he is a very good person, but he is so rough. I feel like he is not connecting to his higher self."

Deva Kaur, my Kundalini Yoga teacher, told me of a mantra (So Purkh) that can help uplift the husband and the marriage. I could hardly wait until the next day to get the tape from her. She said, "The meaning of the mantra is 'My man is pure,' and the purpose of this long mantra is that it will help to bring out the best in your husband, especially if you can visualize and imagine him living in his full potential. This is a way to focus on the positive instead of focusing on his negative habits, and build that positive vibration in yourself, and in him."

The next day I was excited to get the tape and I started immediately to listen and repeat the words on the tape so I could learn the mantra. I concentrated for 20 to 30 minutes, repeating the mantra eleven times. I noticed an immediate difference in my husband. It was as if he had been tranquilized when he came home that evening. I was in the kitchen, and he came and gave me a big hug and a kiss. It felt like the wild lion from the jungle had become a domesticated cat! He was more romantic, and was definitely a lot softer.

I thought "Wow, I am going to play this tape every day," which I did every morning without missing for a long time. Even my housekeeper noticed the difference right away. She said, "That prayer that you play all the time, it makes a big difference in your husband. He's completely a new person." I told her, "See, that's the power of the prayer." I didn't explain to her what a mantra was. I kept playing it and playing it until I knew it by heart.

The benefits of the meditation were multiple. I definitely feel that my husband and I became more intimate as a result of this meditation. I feel that when he got softer, our souls became closer, and it became a beautiful relationship. I also noticed the difference in my son. He got softer, and there was a lot of harmony in the whole house that affected my daughter as well.

Then I stopped doing the mantra, because I thought everything was fixed. But, once in a while, I felt a little roughness starting with our communication, as the unkind words started to reappear. My housekeeper came to me and said, "I think you should start playing that tape again, and doing the prayer/mantra, because it really makes a difference in your husband." So I started again, and I noticed that every time I did the *So Purkh* meditation it made a huge difference in our relationship. It shows me again and again the power of mantra. It is an extremely effective mantra. I feel the mantra seeps into my subconscious mind, and touches me very deeply on a soul level to remind me that I am connected to the Infinite.

I have developed more compassion for my husband's needs, and he has more grace and respect in his communication.

At a certain age, I discovered that old emotions started coming up for both of us. Since we don't need the past anymore, mantra is helping us to clear it. By connecting us to Infinity, these words help us to realize and remember that we are that Infinity and not all the limitations and fears that feel so real. They are an illusion or mirage that the mantra can break through. The use of the mantra helps to liberate you from the negativity of those emotions. The *So Purkh* Meditation helped me to turn my marriage from a nightmare to a dream, from a hell to a heaven. I am very grateful to Yogi Bhajan for sharing this sacred technology with my teacher, so she could share it with me, and I, in turn, shall share it with my yoga students.

WHY STAY MARRIED?

BY HARI BHAJAN KAUR KHALSA · LOS ANGELES, CA

THERE IS NO MAKING SENSE OF WHY he and I still eat at the same breakfast table, sleep on the same mattress, work out plans for next year and the one after that. Oh, it is totally comprehensible why we first got together. He was cute, blond, with a bit of a mustache, wearing blue jean overalls with the vibe of farm kid mixed with "Rebel without a cause." Irresistible, at least to me, who hadn't had much luck in love since letting the high school boyfriend go when our paths set in opposite directions. Yes, at 19 there were hormones involved (little did we know), but, as my numerologist said many years later, "The two of you have been linked together for many lifetimes." Brother and sister? Or perhaps I was his mother or he the master to my slave. Nevertheless, she says we are "as bound as four hands tightly crossed and held."

We didn't know each other those first few years of marriage. We hardly knew ourselves. Like a genie in a bottle there was so much we kept inside, while only smoky whiffs escaped when one of us tried to pry the lid off. It wasn't that we didn't want to know each other. We just didn't know we needed to know. We were busy. We had to maintain a home, pay the bills, go to yoga class, work several jobs at once (cleaning offices, running a sandwich shop, planting fledgling trees, hauling garbage from summer campgrounds). We had to get-by and move-on.

We took a trip to L.A. that lasted 28 years. He went to chiropractic school, finished in '82 and is still showing up every day at the office. I worked, put him through school, raised a child (through potty training, the India program, rebellious teens and world-wide wanderings), as well as searched for my own place in the planetary scheme. We were busy. Did I already say that?

We have a lot of differences. I want to vacation in the Caribbean, lie on the beach, read and contemplate the turning planet. He plans a weekend at Yosemite in the dead of winter to stay in the Awahnee Lodge (#23 on his "100-things-I-must-do-before-I-die" list). I want to visit museums, shop, play cards and read poetry. He spends Sunday afternoons watching the Yankees or Raiders, buys a collapsible kayak, periodically proposes we sell our house, get a motor home and roam the country for a few years.

Is it like this in all marriages? I have no idea. I've never been married to anyone else. I have seen those TV shows where real-life couples ride bikes together in Belize or hoist the sails in their sailboat named "Forever," or behold Greek sculpture all while holding hands, smiling into each other's shining faces declaring, "We do everything together. We can't imagine it any other way." I really can't imagine it that way. We do have our joint bank account, IRA's and local mailing address. We drive the same make of car and get teary eyed when we hear the Moody Blues play our song. We like to go for long drives and talk about moving to a place where pine trees shed three-pronged needles and the sky has a million stars. After we meditate together our voices soften, our hands reach to massage, and we laugh about silly things.

You try to make it work, beyond all the odds—two people, born at different latitude and longitude, separate species of the human race, clumping along on two feet, hearts beating at different rates, each with an enormous brain full of God-only-knows-what kind of rot designed to tear you away from each other, to make you stand up and scream to the other, "Me, me! It's about ME!"

Maybe we've given up on trying to mold each other to our own specifications. Maybe now we prefer that the other feel safe, supported. We now dare to reveal our fears and find that they are not as far apart as we had once believed. Chasing the truth in oneself, in the other, in the marriage is an elusive, snakelike creature. At one moment it looks hard and fast, the next it slithers across your consciousness sideways and you see its fluidity, its ability to shape shift right before your eyes.

My husband and I have not solved all our problems, but we are forgetting more and more that we have them. We are not perfect, but the picture of perfect has grown murky, taken on a surrealistic pattern and tone. We aren't sure if we are "in love" anymore. What we are sure of is that on a winter day over 30 years ago we vowed to hold the hand of the other, even should our heads roll, and though our heads have rolled this way and that a thousand times over the years, one of us has always reached out a hand to catch it and return it to the other. And then we have walked on. We will always walk on, together.

THE RIGHT ANSWER
SIRI PRITAM KAUR KHALSA · YUBA CITY, CA

Dear Shakti Parwha Kaur,

Sat Nam. Pritam Singh and I got married at the beautiful Hargobind Sadan Ashram in San Rafael, California on September 22, 1974, following a Teachers' Training course. We had known each other three weeks. He passed away on April 26, 2002, here at Mukande Ashram in Yuba City, California.

It was over thirty years ago...he came in from Austin, Texas, for our Teacher's Training course. I had been living at the San Rafael ashram for only a few months. We just barely took notice of one another, but it must have shown. Yogiji was coming to town for a White Tantric weekend. A couple of phone calls to him by the director of the Ashram, Karam Jot Singh, and suddenly word was, we were going to get married that Sunday!

It was all put together quickly: Jagdish arranged a bed of flowers on a $50 budget. Guru Terath Kaur made whole-wheat sweet rolls and Yogi Tea. The Sat Kirtans, Vikram and Sada Anand Singh played kirtan.[70]

That Sunday morning, we were sitting in front of the Guru[71]—one didn't walk around the Guru yet for the ceremony in those early years—waiting for Yogiji to come downstairs to officiate. He took a long time. It seemed like an hour. When he finally came, it was clear he wasn't going to make this easy. Right away he asked me, "What is the ONE thing that is going to break your marriage?" I was fairly new at this, having had only eight months of ashram life, so I wasn't sure what to say. The entire ceremony came to a stand still. "What is the one thing that will break your marriage?!?"

The best I could think of was, 'If you don't love God?' His answer was quick and sharp as a knife— "Leave God out of this! What is the one thing that will break your marriage?"

Again I kept looking for the right answer, for what he wanted. I tried, "If you don't love one another?" "Love has nothing to do with it. What is the ONE thing that will break your marriage?!?"

I was getting quite desperate; since it was clear he wasn't going to continue until he had the answer he wanted. Finally, realizing I was going nowhere, I admitted, "I don't know.'

"You Americans. You always say 'I don't know,' as if that was an answer. The thing that is going to break your marriage is (and he paused, a long pause)—a clash of EGOS. That's what will break your marriage."

The ceremony proceeded. I did get the point and haven't forgotten to this day. He then made us promise to live as Sikhs. He made us promise to bring our children up as Sikhs. In essence, we were taking our Sikh vows right there and then.

Editor's Note: In 1994, after 20 years of marriage (and three children), Pritam Singh wrote this beautiful poem to his wife:

TIES

Your hold on me grows stronger day by day.
At the same time it grows ever more soft and subtle.
Your presence is always with me,
But it is lighter with each passing hour.

We have gone through much together, you and I,
Pushing, pulling, occasionally battling,
Like two rafts tied together with a long rope,
Pulling this way and that in barely coordinated attempt
To cross the world ocean.

I have always felt your fetters of love
Provoking, calling
My every action.

Lately, though, I sometimes don't feel them at all,
Only recognizing your touch
After I have done what I wanted to do.

Your wants, needs, and aspirations
Have mixed with mine.
Now we go along together, you and I,
In a straighter course,
Helping each other onward,
But mostly cruising easily side by side.

Pritam Singh Khalsa, September 1994

You should only consider yourself married when you are on the death bed. If, by that time, the husband is still there, shake hands with him and declare yourself married, otherwise there is no such thing as marriage—it doesn't exist.

Yogi Bhajan, KWTC 1979

MARITAL ART

GURUMUSTUK SINGH KHALSA · ESPANOLA, NM

Gurumustuk Singh and Arjan Kaur were married January 3, 1999. When he wrote this he was 30 and she was 31. They met at Winter Solstice, 1996.

I HAVE BEEN MARRIED FOR SIX YEARS and feel very lucky to have a wonderful marriage. It's definitely not a piece of cake, though. It really does take both people being committed and willing to work with each other no matter what comes up. For me marriage provides mutual support, stability and companionship. Being married is like a spiritual path, which teaches you many lessons and allows you to challenge each other to work on yourself and be a better person.

I look at a person's life as having different levels of challenge/mastery, which are like Karate belts:

- ‣ White belt: Single Person
- ‣ Brown belt: Married
- ‣ Black belt: Married with Children

Being Married with Children is the ultimate level, with many challenges and tests to learn from (along with the many joys that come along with it).

Here are some key areas that have been keys to my successful marriage:

COMMUNICATION

For my wife and me communication has been the KEY. You really have to talk to each other and listen to what the other person is saying. Acknowledge their feelings and make sure they feel that you understand them. Marriage is a partnership; it's not all about you.

ACKNOWLEDGEMENT

I see many wives who do so much taking care of their husbands and children, and the household, as well as working a full time job. In many cases the wives are frustrated and overwhelmed. It is so important to help each other out and not be lazy. The biggest thing you can do is to at least take the time to appreciate your spouse. If you do this they will love you even more, and feel really good about doing those things. When you don't show appreciation or help out, resentment can come in and feelings of not being supported. Every time my wife makes me a meal or does something for me I thank her and make sure I tell her how delicious the food was. She loves to cook for me because she knows it means a lot to me and she gets well appreciated.

FINANCES

I used to deal with all the finances in our household, but the problem was my wife had no concept of how much money we had, and how easily it was spent. Women love to buy things, even more than guys like electronics. I know many wives spend money as fast as they make it. I found the key is to make the woman of the house responsible for the finances. That way she learns to relate to the money. This turned our finances from "just getting by" every month to saving a lot of money.

ARGUMENTS

If you have an argument or fight, don't run off or leave things unfinished. You need to get closure and work things out. It's okay to take a few minutes to think about things or cool down, but you don't want to slam the door and take off in an angry burst. Feelings of anger and frustration will just grow and grow till they ruin your marriage. Don't bottle things up, talk about them and work something out.

COMPROMISE AND CHANGE

Couples have different things in their household life that are important, but in most cases they are small things. Things like cleaning up after your self, putting the toilet seat down, arranging the house in a certain way. Don't resist change on these small things. I have found that if I just adapt and do the small things that are important to my wife it makes a huge difference. Then when there are things that are important to me I let her know and she adapts and changes to my needs. It is a give and take.

ROMANCE

We live in a busy fast moving age. You come home, eat dinner, maybe watch TV and then go to sleep. It is too easy to lose the romance that is such a binding force for a marriage. As a guy I know it is hard to do the romantic stuff, but women NEED this. If you don't take the time to do fun things, surprise her, do things which make her feel loved and appreciated, you'll be in trouble. I used to give excuses about many of the holidays being so commercial and not wanting to buy into it. My wife let me get away with it for a while. The problem was that I didn't do much in place of those holidays. Finally she said that she didn't care if they were commercial holidays, and that she expected flowers, cards, gifts, surprises. Men: it's worth the effort!

From the day I met Arjan she has been an inspiration to me, and loves me for who I am. I remember coming back from India after going to school there, not having many friends, trying to fit in, and be something that I was not. When I met Arjan we had a connection right away. She had recently become a Sikh. For her the Sikhi lifestyle was what she had been looking for. She turned my life around. I had been having others pressure me to cut my hair, and not wear bana, etc, and it was so refreshing to meet a woman who thought it was so attractive wearing a turban and *bana* (kurta/pajama). For once I could just be me. I always pray that other single Sikhs also meet someone who stretches them to be a better person.

MARRIAGE IS A CARRIAGE...
SIRI ATMA KAUR KHALSA · LOS ANGELES, CA

YOGIJI SAYS, "MARRIAGE IS A CARRIAGE." To the infinite. I suppose he means a true union, a joining of two individuals when all their separateness disappears. Synergy, amalgamation—when a new, more precious substance is created. Is this a rehearsal, a drill, a taste of what the ultimate merger of my soul with God will be?

Now I see the smoothing of a rough surface, a softening of the hard corners that have been carefully polished and sharpened for years. I had unwittingly built these walls (so complicated with obtuse angles) to protect me, to repel, so nothing goes deep into my being. I have kept myself separate, wary and distant, even from my own soul.

In this cozy, safe bubble of marriage my shiny sharp edges have softened, melted. The cage that has surrounded me for so long sublimates, transforming the iron bars into wispy tendrils of smoke. I begin to find my Self, my true voice, and share it, and begin to merge with another being. This is just the beginning of intimacy. In our true union there's no longer a 'you' or a 'me' but a new element that is even beyond "WE". Indescribable, really. Sometimes I feel it. I know he does too. I long for it and relish it.

I can only imagine that ultimate union, the true marriage of my soul with my Creator. Thanks, God, for giving me the opportunity to practice here on earth.

THE SECOND TIME AROUND

DR. SIRI ATMA SINGH KHALSA • ESPANOLA, NM

MARRIAGE IS THE CARRIAGE THAT TAKES YOU TO GOD. This is what Yogi Bhajan taught me in 1979 and it is what I believe now. Trusting in God, I did not pursue a wife, but rather I consolidated my spiritual practice, prepared myself for marriage and let God take care of the rest. When I was married and found that my personal *sadhana* would lead to such rapid personal change that we would grow apart, I set my personal pace to match my spouse's. Thus I verified that personal sacrifice always leads to spiritual growth.

Eventually I was forced to choose between performing my duty and preserving my marriage. Whichever choice I made the personal cost was going to be high. I chose what I felt was the highest good, but I lost a 20 year relationship, my children were forced through a divorce, and my dreams of a single cozy grandparents' home was destroyed. Worse still, my trust in a partnership was destroyed. My distrust made constructing a new union difficult for my new partner, though constant love and nurturing eventually has healed this pain.

I learned that no matter how good or bad a relationship may be, there is no substitute for time spent together. This being said, relationships are a lot easier when you both not only love but also respect each other. With my new partner we have both merged deeper in four years than our prior 20-year marriages afforded. Why? We both already knew how to serve and sacrifice, when to lead or follow. We both know how to heal and strengthen each other.

Creating a new relationship after divorce takes a different set of skills than starting fresh. Besides losing my trust in partnerships, I wasn't sure how much I really wanted or needed a new relationship. The dream of having children and creating a cozy family free of divorce was gone. "What can we do for each other?" became the focus.

We both want with equal intensity to live and share the Siri Singh Sahib's teachings. Our marriage has evolved around healing our wounds and enhancing our strengths. We are both good self-nurturers, but we prefer to nurture each other instead. It is more fun to pass your day-to-day in giving rather than hassling and hustling. The Siri Singh Sahib's teachings are self-applied to grant us the power to serve others as well as each other and ourselves, just as we are.

The Siri Singh Sahib has tested us both and that is nice. We know how to sacrifice and share and when to relax and play. We respect our strengths and our weaknesses. We spend our together time enjoying and expressing our unique identities, not seeking satisfaction of our personal needs.

Our shared commitments built trust, bore intimacy, and then a merging of souls. I feel blessed that the Siri Singh Sahib taught me to commit, trust, and sacrifice. This allowed me to merge with him and it allows me now to merge with my wife, Nam Kaur. A successful marriage requires the same tools as the spiritual path and promises the same rewards, merger of one soul with another, *Atma*[72] into *Parmatma*.[73]

Marriage is not about what I have or what you have. It is not about what I am or what you are. Marriage is about what we can be by joining our polarity. When the goal of marriage is to obey the soul in purity and piety then union must occur, because there is only one Soul. If I merge into my soul or your soul or the highest Soul, it is all one Soul, one Creation. If I live for you and I serve your soul and I merge into your soul, I escape the pit of Spiritual Ego where I serve only my soul.

Marriage is the personal and public declaration that I will serve this other soul unto Infinity. We will sink or swim together. This is the real spiritual test of marriage. It is not our earthly success or failure that pleases God, but our ability to commit and sacrifice. Marriage is thus a practice ground for merging with all souls. We commit to merge with one soul and whatever it takes, that is the sacrifice we make. The secret is to constantly nurture the highest aspect of our sexual polarity, our partner, because it takes two wings to fly.

Dr. Siri Atma Singh served as one of the Siri Singh Sahib's personal physicians. He gave up his personal medical practice to devote himself full-time to the care of his Teacher.

CHOICES
MSS GURUKA SINGH KHALSA

IF YOU LOOK UP THE WORD "MARRIAGE" in Webster's dictionary one of the meanings given is "To blend completely. Ex: Allow the flavors to marry overnight." A good marriage is just that: when two people become completely blended into one.

So what does that mean exactly? Yogi Bhajan said that the husband must be able to speak for the wife, and vice versa. "Let me talk to my husband first and see what he thinks," is just an excuse, a delaying tactic. The wife should know exactly what her husband will say and be able to speak for him without any doubt. That requires a very high degree of effective subtle communication. Such communication is really telepathic in nature.

After 35 years of marriage, I can tune into my wife and know what she is thinking and feeling whether she is physically present or not.

Shakti asked me to give some advice about marriage, so my advice is as follows. Just as with everything else in your life, whatever you pay attention to grows and prospers, and what you ignore dies away. Pay attention to the divinity in your spouse; to what is best and most beautiful. To what you admire and appreciate the most. Ignore the rest. Your spouse will become more and more divine in his or her words and actions. Ignore the things that may bother or annoy you, and simply don't give them the blessing of your attention or your energy.

Marriage is all about keeping up and confronting your self. Why do people get divorced? Most of the time, it has nothing to do with the other person. It is because one person cannot get straight with him or herself and move to the next level of spiritual growth that is required. It is so much easier to blame the other person than to look in the mirror and confront your own demons. So the person ends up saying "The marriage didn't work out." That is bullshit. You didn't grow up to the level required of you!

Marriage is all about keeping up and working on your self. It is the cauldron that cooks you; the highest ashram of all. You can't work on your spouse. You can only work on yourself. But you can support each other in that work. Therein lies the blessing.

Once Yogi Bhajan told a story; he said, "When you are on your deathbed, take hold of your spouse's hand, and at that time, and only at that time, as you breathe your last breath can you say, 'we are truly married.'"

So keep up. Open your heart. Pay attention to the divinity and beauty of your spouse and feel the blessings in your life every day. Do not focus on the insufficiencies but only on the blessings. Let prosperity, love, and beauty rule your life. Live each day with an attitude of gratitude.

Remember, it is always your choice what you choose to pay attention to. That is what will shape your life and your marriage.

Teacher, writer and inveterate punster MSS Guruka Singh Khalsa is the Executive Director of www.SikhNet.com In this incarnation, he met Yogi Bhajan in 1971, began teaching Kundalini Yoga, and has taught ever since. He translated Yogi Bhajan's Gurmukhi poetry into English for the volume *Furmaan Khalsa* and translated Guru Nanak's *Japji* and other hymns from Sikh scriptures. Known by many as Doctor Hi-Fi, Guruka loves to play with electronics, computers and words. He is one of the founders of Sun & Son, a cutting edge consulting firm.

HUSBANDS AND WIVES
YOGI BHAJAN & BIBIJI'S STORY

IN 1953, AT AGE TWENTY-FOUR, then an Indian Government Customs Officer, Harbhajan Singh Puri, later to be known as Yogi Bhajan, married Bibi Inderjit Kaur. Because of his official responsibility, immediately after the wedding Yogiji had to present a case before the court, so he left his young bride at the Gurdwara with her older sister while he went to attend his duty. That night, there was a wedding party with 500 guests, but the next day he had to leave his bride again when he was called out for official business that lasted until noon the next day. Thus began a marriage that has continued to hold duty as sacred, and recognize it as the highest expression of love.

Bibiji was born to a mother and father who were known for their spiritual strength and compassionate kindness. Yogiji was the grandson of an acknowledged yogi and saint and was guided by him from the time he was born. Yogiji recognized in Bibiji generations of service and devotion and understood her great capacity for sacrifice, which would be called on as they grew together to the fulfillment of their destiny.

Early in their relationship he would listen as she recited her prayers each morning, a discipline she had practiced since childhood. As Yogiji grew to be more recognized for his spiritual insights, many people would call on him for guidance and instruction and Bibiji, ever his support, would serve them food, hospitality, and love.

With a growing understanding of what the future would require of them, they prepared themselves and their three children for a life of service and sacrifice for the mission of spreading Sikh Dharma to the West. They would talk about the time when they would dedicate themselves to serving this mission but they had no idea how soon it would come or how much it would take. Yet, through half a lifetime of separation, test, and challenge they maintained a vibrant and lively relationship, founded on duty and service but based on the loving understanding that all things come from God and all things go to God.

TWO UNITS

YOGI BHAJAN, PH.D.
SIRI SINGH SAHIB OF SIKH DHARMA

LIFE MOVES LIKE A STAR ON A TRACK. It moves on its axle and in its orbit, and it is all nothing but the electro-magnetic field in which two people meet to walk the track together. Without the consideration of good and bad, right and wrong, real and unreal, the unison tracking the passage is called Marriage. It consists of two units. One is called wife; the other is called husband. It is the integrity, personality, the divinity and the dignity of being together which meets. It is the forgiveness, kindness and grace, which keeps us going. It is the beauty, the bounty and the blessings, which make the marriage strong.

All these years of life as we have walked and as God has guided us to be, we are grateful in gratitude that we could accomplish a state of mind that we can serve people, love them, elevate them to their own greatness. We both feel as gardeners the wonderful fragrance of the flower. It is our reward and success, our beauty, our unison, our ecstasy and our children and grandchildren, as they are our future.

A WIFE'S PERSPECTIVE
BY SIRI SARDARNI BHAI SAHIBA BIBIJI INDERJIT KAUR PHD
CHIEF RELIGIOUS MINISTER SIKH DHARMA OF THE WESTERN HEMISPHERE

BEING MARRIED TO YOGI BHAJAN was a divine blessing from God. When people are young, they are very concerned about being physically together. As they grow older, they become cozy within their unity and there is a deep understanding in the silence of the unspoken word. In later stages of life, it is the merge of the glance, a harmony of their intuitive sense with the divine ecstasy of the God within.

Being married to a man of peace and a world religious leader has given me the opportunity to live a beautiful full life. I feel deep gratitude for all the great calm and cool reflections of the moon and for memories of joy, happiness, and wonderful times. My prayers have been answered and I have served by my husband's side to bring peace on Earth through coziness in the home and the remembrance of God within each being.

The reality of life has served the totality of purpose for my gracious God who has stood with me. My beloved Guru has cared for me and guided me in my lonely moments when the caravan of life passed through valleys of calamities, cruel times, and fierce battles, and He guided the caravan safely home and joyful in love. Now before us we have the beautiful living mission of our great destiny: the Sovereign Khalsa Spiritual Nation.

ABOUT THE AUTHOR: HOW I MET YOGI BHAJAN
BY SHAKTI PARWHA KAUR KHALSA

THEY SAY LIFE BEGINS AT 40. Well, my life as Shakti Parwha Kaur Khalsa began when I met Yogi Bhajan about six months before my 40th birthday. It didn't occur to me that I might be going through "mid-life crisis," but my 19-year-old son was certainly in crisis. He had tried to commit suicide, and then gone AWOL from the Army at Fort Ord, California. I didn't know where he was. He had written that he was planning to go to Canada, as many young men were doing. I was worried that if he left the country he would lose his U.S. citizenship, something I value highly.

I had just met Yogi Bhajan, and at dinner in a restaurant with 6 other people, he leaned across the table and said, "Your son's in trouble, isn't he?" I said, "Yes, he is." This unknown yogi told me, "There is nothing more powerful than the prayer of a mother for her son." And, "If you will chant *EK ONG KAR SAT NAM SIRI WHA GURU* for one hour every morning before sunrise, and pray for your son, he will be all right." To make a long story short (a story I've told elsewhere[74]), it worked. And thus began my apprenticeship with the extraordinary Teacher of teachers, who was to become world famous. In 1971, Yogi Bhajan was appointed the Chief Religious and Administrative Authority for Sikh Dharma of the Western Hemisphere; he was The Man Called the Siri Singh Sahib.[75]

Yogi Bhajan and I sat on the floor of my Los Angeles apartment looking in the phone book for YMCA's where he might be able to teach classes in Kundalini Yoga. He had realized during that weekend in December of 1968 that Los Angeles was a Mecca for the generation of youth searching for the experience of God. He knew that taking drugs would destroy their health, whereas the practice of Kundalini Yoga would give them a valid experience—and help heal the wounds of their minds and bodies.

I drove him to the classes he taught. Sitting at his feet, I took notes and acted as his assistant. He spent hours and hours talking with me, answering my questions. I told him everything about my life: my parents' divorce when I was five, my father's suicide when I was 12, my marriage at 18, my son's birth at 20, and my divorce at 22. I explained that I had discovered Astrology, which helped to answer the pesky "Why me?" question. My horoscope showed the challenges I had chosen to face and the lessons I needed to learn in this lifetime, making it clear to me that I could no longer blame anyone else for the events in my life. I accepted the fact that everything that happened was an opportunity for me to work out my karma.[76]

I told Yogi Bhajan that in my search for meaning and purpose in life I had studied with many different teachers, including several Hindu Swamis, and a Sufi Pir. I told him of my trip around the world in 1966, living in India at the Sri Aurobindo Ashram in Pondicherry, after a visit to Bangalore to see Sri Satya Sai Baba. I proudly recited the list of all the books I had read on Eastern Philosophy and Metaphysics.

He said, very kindly, "You know a lot, but I can put it all together for you." I could not imagine then how much he knew, and certainly had no idea how much I had yet to learn!

True to his commitment to train teachers, not gather "disciples," he had me teach my first class in Kundalini Yoga in early 1969 and I have continued teaching ever since, specializing in teaching beginners.

At his direction, I wrote *KUNDALINI YOGA: The Flow of Eternal Power*. Later I put together a *Toolkit for Teaching Beginners Kundalini Yoga*, for 3HO's Teacher Training programs. I created the 3HO in-house newsletter, *The Science of Keeping Up*,[77] wrote two more books, *Kundalini Postures and Poetry*, and *Sun Sign Rhymes and Other Wise Verses: Astrological and Philosophical Observations*.[78] And when the *Aquarian Times* magazine was born in 2000, I became a contributing editor.

By 2004, as a Sikh (I had been ordained as a Sikh minister in 1974), it was obvious to me that a simple book about Sikh Dharma was needed, not written by a scholar or an historian, but rather from a personal standpoint. As an American I have explored many spiritual paths and found that in Sikh Dharma, my soul found its home. I may call the book *Sikh Dharma: Too Bad It's a Religion!* The point I want to make is obvious: religions tend to separate people, spawn fanaticism, and make for aggressive proselytizing, whereas the righteous way of living (*dharma*) that Guru Nanak, the first Sikh Guru, taught, and all his successors expanded upon, is a universal, truly Aquarian path. Sikh Dharma teaches respect for all human beings, and respect for their choice of how to worship the One God who created us all. And, I want to introduce people to the *Shabd Guru*, the Siri Guru Granth Sahib, so they can experience the powerful technology of the sound current of the Words it contains.

Before I go back to working on that, I plan to complete compiling an anthology of Yogi Bhajan's poetry.

Meanwhile, I live happily in Los Angeles, California, close to several "state of the art" movie theaters, which I visit often, and even closer to our 3HO yoga center, Yoga West, where I teach Beginners Kundalini Yoga, do *sadhana*, and cross the street every morning to Guru Ram Das Ashram for the 6 a.m. Gurdwara, where I bask in the vibrations of the *Shabd Guru*, recalling the many times Yogi Bhajan spoke there, inspiring, educating and above all, challenging us to excel, and not to "give distance to our destiny."

You have to be positive. Each one of you has the power to be what
you don't think you are, or what you think you cannot be.
Siri Singh Sahib Ji

TEN CHARACTERISTICS OF LOVE

1. Love is blind, it never sees anything.

2. Love is infinite. What you hear is not worth anything,
what is worthwhile you don't have to hear.

3. Love is in silence and deep sound, it has no words.

4. When you are in love, you neither see, nor hear, nor speak.

5. You experience your partner as yourself.

6. Within yourself lies the grace,
which you can feel in the projection of your mate.

7. Love is amalgamation—not adjustment.

8. Love is sublimation—not a gross understanding.

9. Love is a distillation and not a relation of feelings or emotions.

10. Love is a consciousness and intelligence —
living in another being and experiencing yourself.

*"If you can even understand these ten points,
then feel that you are married—you are married in love."*

Yogi Bhajan • Spring • 1989

CHAPTER THIRTEEN

THE WEDDING

"...They will be renewed by the memory of the beautiful moments of the wedding, love, romance, and their togetherness through the years. It is a moment of sharing, fulfillment in divinity, joy and happiness in Grace in the most spiritual atmosphere of blessings and preciousness of the life to which we all look forward in this moment of festivity."

Quote from the Siri Singh Sahib (Yogi Bhajan) on a wedding invitation, 1994

 EDDING VOWS

Nowadays some couples want to write their own wedding vows.

They may come up with something eloquent, sincere, and emotionally satisfying. But for sheer inspiration and caliber, I don't think you can beat the vows that Guru Ram Das wrote for his own wedding over four hundred years ago. What is a vow? It is a sacred promise. It is a promise you make to God. The elevated consciousness with which Guru Ram Das spoke goes to the very heart and soul of this sacred bond. Called *Lavan*, his "Wedding Song" outlines the essential steps of the marriage commitment. These core values are timeless.

In the Sikh wedding ceremony, the four verses of the *Lavan* are read one at a time.  The first round is read from the Siri Guru Granth Sahib in the original Gurmukhi. Then a translation is read in English or whatever the native language might be. After each round is read, the couple bows to the Shabd Guru in acceptance of the instruction just given. Then the musicians play and sing the words of the round in Gurmukhi as the couple stand and walk clockwise around the Guru.

The Guru is the beginning, the middle, and the pivot of a sacred marriage. The bride holds on to one end of a shawl, which has been draped around the groom's shoulders. She doesn't let go! This symbolizes the connection between them. When they return to their places in front of the Guru, they bow together and sit down again to listen to the next round of instruction.

You can read the English translation of the *Lavan* below, followed by commentary about each round, based on what one Minister said at a ceremony held at Guru Ram Das Ashram in Los Angeles. Keep in mind that when the Lavan was written (about 400 years ago) most people were very familiar with the Vedas and Brahma,[79] to which Guru Ram Das refers, as well as the Smritis, ancient sacred scriptures, which he mentions.

LAVAN: THE WEDDING SONG
GURU RAM DAS

THE FIRST ROUND
"Proceeding forth into the first nuptial round
The Lord presents before you His instruction for
The daily duties of marital life:
It is not enough to relate to the Vedas or Brahma,
You must be constant in the performance of your righteous duty,
Thus the errors of the past shall be washed away.

Be confirmed in righteousness and
Repeat the Lord's Name.
The practice of the Name has been urged in the Smritis as well.
Reflect upon the True Guru, who is ever perfect,
And all your sins and errors will leave you.
By the greatest good fortune the mind is filled with bliss
And thoughts of the Lord are soothing to the mind.
Slave Nanak proclaims that in this first round,
The marriage ceremony has begun."

The First Round represents the Past.

Guru is instructing you what to do to be free of all your past. Guru says relating to ancient scriptures or some deities is not enough, you have to meditate on God's Name (*Simran*), and be of service (*Seva*) to the community as well as to the Guru. By being committed to your spiritual path and keeping up consistently in your daily spiritual practice, *sadhana*, "...all your sins and errors will leave you." This works because *Simran* and *Seva* are powerful practices that can bring you back to an elevated state of consciousness. This allows you to recognize mistakes, learn from them, and move on.

THE SECOND ROUND

"Comes the second nuptial round
And the Lord has made you to meet the True Guru.
With your heart bound by the fear of the Fearless God,
All sense of pride has been washed from the mind.
Knowing the fear of God and singing His praises,
You behold His presence before you.
God, the Lord Master, is the soul of the creation,
He pervades everywhere and fills all places with His Being.
Know then that there is One God, within us and without,
And His songs of rejoicing are heard in the company of His servants.
Nanak proclaims that in this second nuptial round, the Divine Music is heard."

This Second Round represents the Present.

Here you are, right this minute, in the presence of Guru, experiencing an opportunity toward which your entire life has been leading. Whatever happened in the past has brought you to this very moment; now you can drop it! You have been transformed into beings free of the past, living completely in the now.

Feel the presence of the Infinite God everywhere, in every particle, in every sound, with every breath. It is in this state of complete awareness of the moment that one can have the experience of the Infinite while in finite form. This is true yoga.

There is no place where God is not. See God in each other. Recognizing the divine in all is the key to maintaining a neutral and non-reactive mind.

Having completed this round, you are now free to move on.

The Third Round

"In the third round the praises of the Lord fill my mind.

By the greatest good fortune you have come to meet the Lord God

in the company of the holy.

Singing His praises and speaking the Divine Word, the Immaculate Lord is found.

It is by very great good fortune

That the pious attain to the Lord

And tell that story which can never be told!

The music of God resounds within and we contemplate the Lord God,

For we have been blessed with a great destiny written upon our foreheads.

Slave Nanak proclaims that in this third round, the love of God

has been awakened in the heart."

This Third Round represents the Future.

It is not an accident or a matter of chance that the two of you are here today in the House of Guru Ram Das. Lifetimes of service and sacrifice have brought you to this point and have earned you the privilege of making this sacred commitment together.

This commitment is made now, for the future, and unto Infinity: To live with the complete focus that together you shall attain to and fulfill your highest destiny. There is a great peace and sense of secure enduring love in knowing that your marriage is much more than any material or physical needs. It is your shared higher purpose that shall sustain and uplift you. Know that your every act and projection shall have its effect upon the future. Live consciously. Never utter a harsh word; it cannot be unspoken. Never act in a way that you will regret. Live in kindness. Raise your children to be givers, heroes, saints, to create a secure and divine future.

THE FOURTH ROUND

"In this fourth round,
The mind grasps the knowledge of the Divine,
And God is realized within.
By the Guru's Grace, we have reached the Lord with ease.
Our bodies and our souls are filled
With the tender delight of the Beloved.
I am a sacrifice unto my Lord.
God seems sweet to me and I have become pleasing to my Master.
He fills my thoughts all night and day.

I have obtained the object of my heart's desire—my Lord.
By praising His name I have gained the highest praise.
The Lord Himself becomes one with His Holy bride,
While the heart of the bride blooms and flowers with His Holy Name.
Slave Nanak proclaims that in the fourth round we have found the Eternal Lord."

This Fourth Round completes the circle, ties the knot, and creates a bond unto Infinity.

As you complete this round, the *sadh sangat* (congregation/company of the holy) will shower you with flower petals. The flower petals represent all the blessings that come to you as your hearts open and are filled with the love of God.

Your challenge, and your gift, is to live and fulfill your duties on earth while at the same time being absorbed in God. Feet on the ground, head in the heavens. In this state, you have the awareness that you are a drop of water in the vast Ocean of the Infinite: indistinguishable yet unique, tasting the joy of complete balance.

A complete divine union is experienced through a spiritual marriage. Understanding this, choosing this path unto Infinity, you bow to Siri Guru Granth Sahib, and the final round is completed.

WEDDING GUEST?

Have you been invited to a wedding? Do you think that it really doesn't matter whether you go or not? Think again!

> *"Blessed are those who come to share the prayer of the young couple to send them with blessings on the path of Life. The art and the start of their new life is an auspicious experience."*
>
> Yogi Bhajan

A wedding ceremony creates a sacred space, whether it's in a Church, a synagogue, a mosque, a Gurdwara, or outdoors in a park. When you're there you have the opportunity to reaffirm your faith in God. If you're already married, you may be inspired to recapture and deepen the commitment you felt when you first took your wedding vows.

A wedding is a sacred, inspiring occasion. I am very fond of Sikh weddings. I hope you can attend one sometime. Although there is a basic structure and sequence to the Ceremony, each wedding is very personal and unique. Often it's a lot of fun, and there can be a lot of laughter. It all depends upon the minister and what is appropriate for the couple.

A NON-SIKH WEDDING

Recently one of the students taking the Kundalini Yoga Teacher Training Course at Yoga West in Los Angeles asked me if I would consider being the minister at her wedding. The couple wanted a "spiritual" ceremony, not a religious one. She said she and her fiancé didn't follow any particular religion.

So, I agreed. Actually I welcomed the opportunity to share the wisdom of Guru Ram Das' wedding vows, which are valuable for people of any religion. I took the translation of the *Lavan* from *Peace Lagoon* and spent some time (actually a lot of time) editing it for the occasion.

It was a pleasant, sunny California afternoon. The ceremony took place outdoors in a small amphitheater in a park, with the guests sitting in bleachers. Rather than ask the expected, "If anyone objects to this marriage…" I asked if the congregation agreed to the marriage, which seemed much more important to establish. And they shouted their enthusiastic approval. I explained how important the support of family and friends will be to the couple. Considering that the bride had two sets of parents attending (both parents had remarried), I called all four of them to come up, along with the groom's original set, and stand with the couple for the opening prayer.

I divided the ceremony into four segments, based on the four rounds of the *Lavan*: Past, Present, Future, and Infinity. I elaborated on each section, challenging the couple to agree to each pledge. If you've read this book so far, you pretty much know what I said about dropping the past; committing to a daily spiritual practice; realizing that whatever they say or do affects the future, and throughout, knowing that the ultimate goal of marriage – and life, is to merge with the Infinite. Having just been working on this book, I included plenty of quotes about marriage from Yogi Bhajan.

Although the ceremony went well, and I was thanked profusely, I have to say, for me personally, it's much easier, and feels more complete, to conduct a Sikh wedding. There is nothing to compare with being in the sacred space of a Gurdwara, with *kirtan* playing, and the Guru presiding. However, I know that because I didn't say "No," the guests, most of whom had probably never even met a Sikh before, have now heard the Guru's universal teachings about the sanctity of marriage.

I feel blessed when given any opportunity to share this wisdom—wisdom that is surely needed in today's world of casual relationships, multiple divorces, broken promises and broken hearts.

ANOTHER SIKH MINISTER'S ADVICE

JUNE 19, 2005 • RAM DAS PURI

Excerpts from the wedding of Hari Kaur Khalsa and Sat Sangat Singh Khalsa,
conducted by SS Sat Bachan Kaur Khalsa:[80]

▸ "When this ceremony is carried over as a blueprint for daily life, then this union becomes confident, compassionate and infinite…

▸ "…Of course, life has its challenges. When you live with someone, the good, the bad, and the indifferent become visible and viable…

▸ "Guru gives the gift of clarity to dissolve the enemies of marriage: commotion, blaming, claiming, and attachment to ego…

▸ "…The technology given to us by the Siri Singh Sahib Ji allows us to trade in our scared and scarred personalities for sacred trust. In God we Trust. In Truth we dwell. We are blessed to recognize that all situations are God's Will. Everything He gives us is our blessing. When we have that depth of understanding, we can live for each other and not at each other. Our only duty is to act righteously and with the right attitude. We are not to judge what God's Will brings. We are only to judge what *our* attitude and consciousness *project*…

▸ "…Our happiness is dependent only on our own consciousness, not our circumstances.

▸ Feelings are for the finite. Consciousness is for the Infinite. Living in this state of mind will give any relationship the opportunity to elevate.

▸ Yogi Bhajan said: "God lives in the heart of the faithful. Our soul is our only strength. Consciousness is our only friend."

▸ He also said, "Don't expect anything, then marriage will work. When you expect nothing, you get everything."

"So what is being said here is that this is not a marriage of two people, rather this is a marriage of Consciousness and Guru. When you take one step towards the Guru, He takes a million steps towards you."

CHAPTER FOURTEEN

YOGI BHAJAN CONDUCTS A WEDDING

N ow read what Yogi Bhajan (Siri Singh Sahib Ji) said when he conducted Sat Bachan Kaur's wedding to Hari Jiwan Singh in 1986. He did not mince words! He was very direct, extremely personal and absolutely challenging.

Siri Singh Sahib Ji: Produce yourself. Do you understand the status of this marriage?

Hari Jiwan Singh Khalsa: Yes, Sir.

Do you understand that you are American?

(Yes, Sir.)

Do you understand that you have no value for marriage and that you are Americans?

(Yes, Sir.)

Do you understand that you have no value for marriage and that you only believe in divorce

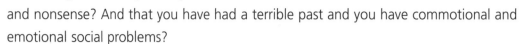

and nonsense? And that you have had a terrible past and you have commotional and emotional social problems?

(Yes Sir.)

Do you understand that you have lost your character? You womanize openly. You leave people in the lurch. You do not raise your children. You are worse than the animals and birds or any creature on the planet. And do you understand that you are holding the hand of this woman before the Siri Guru Granth and that she is holding your hand before the Siri Guru Granth and it is now different?

(Yes, Sir.)

I will give you a few minutes to decide if you emotionally cannot live with this woman tomorrow or if she cannot live with you and if you can lay down this garbage, which is your national property. You had better decide it now before you ask me to continue, because I told you not to ask me to administer this oath of marriage. But because you insisted, and because I have lived in this garbage for nine years and I have loved you, I am doing it.

I know you are very intelligent, very beautiful, I also know you have a terrible past. I am not going to tell the whole story in front of you. I do not know what hell she has been living in. But here I want you to decide as a man and a woman, as a male and a female, as two human beings who are honest enough and truthful enough to look at each other and decide once and for all: is this going to be an emotional, sexual situation or are you going to hold each other's hand till eternity, as good humans? Otherwise what is the use of bringing in God? Go and have a bathroom and a bedroom and whatever you want to do and live your life! All the ceremony is totally unnecessary.

Let us face the facts. If she is going to do her number on you tomorrow and you are going to do your number on her, what's the point? You know you both look very pretty. You're very well dressed at this moment, right? You want to be united and perfect. But this is the moment that we must face you. You waited about two weeks for that, right? (*Laughing*) Yeah? You want to marry? Fine. You understand each other? Fine. You have talked to each other? Fine. You have all the chances on this planet, right? Well, now is my chance. I'm not going to get into tomorrow's emotional problems, and the children will be orphaned, divorce and all that nonsense. Forget it, man! What's that worth? There are 450 million people who go to bed without food every night. You people love to overthrow things. So you overthrow marriages too. But you are the sickest people on this planet at the moment, and I'm not going to make this marriage so that it can be part of the 58% divorce rate of tomorrow. That's what I'm saying. Do you hear me?

(Yes, Sir.)

Well, talk to each other; don't look at me! You have to talk to each other. These people are all your friends. They are not your enemies. They have come to understand this whole nonsense. Otherwise they would have not have taken the trouble to be here and we would not have celebrated this marriage before the Siri Guru Granth Sahib.

If you fail in your promise because you cannot honor your word, then you are no use at all. Get up now and go to that church on the corner. The guy there will marry you right away! I don't want to bring Jesus Christ and Jehovah and God and Allah and all the prophets and everything into the play when people are just going to do their berserk things!

I don't care who the hell you are. I just want to know exactly where your head is at before I play any part in this. Man, I have been telling this truth for nine years! Nobody listens to me. God knows whether you have listened to me so far or not.

HJSK: I'm totally committed to this woman, this Dharma. It is my prayer that…

SSS Ji: You know you are going to catch her hand and only after death will you let it go, come what may! You are a MALE; don't play the part, "Because SHE didn't do it!" I'm not going to listen to that tomorrow.

HJSK: I understand, Sir.

You are intelligent enough. I'm just trying to play very fair with you. I believe you come from a good family. You had a good education and you played a foolish role somewhere in between, and if you had had somebody to control you, all you needed was a few spankings and you'd have run straight. But that didn't happen and you did what you wanted to do. *Now is the time* that has put you right before the altar to play the number. Right?

(Yes, Sir.)

You played and you thought you'd be free, right? Nobody can tell you anything because you are an adult. If you are going to leave this woman because somebody very pretty comes along and does a number on you and she says she is your "soul partner"… you understand what I mean? I have heard all those stories, man! There is a whole record of it. With a lot of people. I don't want that thing to happen to you, okay?

(Yes, Sir, absolutely.)

Sure. *(Laughing)* I mean that's the end of it!

(No question, the question does not arise.)

Now raise both your hands up to the sky. That means you surrender. You'll be honest to this woman and you'll be honest to yourself.

(Sat Bachan Kaur raised her arms too; everyone laughs.)

All right. *(SSS Ji laughs)* Arms down. What I mean is that I'm asking you both: are you going to be very honest to each other and live as a male and a female and live very truthful lives, or do you want to play some game?

I can give you a couple of weeks more. We can do it all over again. You know what I mean? You have come all the way from Canada to do it, right? What about you?

(HJSK: Absolutely, Sir.) *(laughter in Sangat)*

Do you have any reservations at this moment?

(None whatsoever.)

Any argument, any logic?

(I've been through all the arguments. *(Sangat laughs)* They are all gone.)

Okay, that's enough. Okay, we agree. Then both of you please bow. Take hold of this cloth properly. You each hold one end. And that means, *"Palai tendai lagee ..."* You are bound by this shawl...

...I'm not a weak man. I don't shut out people, or make them run away because I have held them in faith of God. It is not my job to let them go. They can go. Everybody is free. In our congregation we don't convert anybody. We don't force anybody. But we have reason to explain how to be a human being. That is the purpose of life. That you must understand. You must understand the experience of it and experience it in a way that you can relate to God. Not emotionally, not commotionally, not neurotically, and not because you have to do it. You do not have to marry him and he does not have to marry you. There's no obligation. But it becomes an obligation when you have given your word. Then you must.

"In the beginning was the Word. The Word was with God, and the Word was God." Then live to your word as God. Honor it as God, and die for it! And if there is anything else then there are a lot of other places where you can marry each other. That's what I'm saying in very plain words, because you both are super-intelligent people and I don't want any reservations at this time and I don't want to listen to any garbage tomorrow. Do you understand?

(HJS: Yes, Sir.)

...I think as human beings you have been given enough chance to intelligently understand each other and to make it a most beautiful, living example so that others who are messing around can understand. That's the purpose of life. You know there is nothing equal to you as a woman and a man. You are the spirit and he is the projection. You are the 'fe-' and he is the male. Because I tell you, it is not an equality. If the woman can get pregnant and deliver the baby and the man then has to breastfeed the baby, then the problem can be solved, we don't need the Equal Rights Amendment at all. That way the nature does it! You have to become pregnant. You have to raise the baby. You have to raise the man. You have to raise his future. You have to give him faith. You have to give him feelings and you have to give him character. And you, if you don't give him character... God, there's nothing on this planet you can ever do! And there will be another mess-around situation for which 3HO doesn't even have a budget. It's getting over budget. *(Laughing)* You know that is what worries me most! We started with a definite budget that we are going to take the drug problem out of this country and help the young people live a reasonable life, we are going to make them responsible, and we are running over budget! What I'm saying is: I don't want to spend any of my time or money or any telephone calls or anything counseling this marriage! Is that clear?

(Yes, Sir.)

I want to be very straight on that. *(Laughing)* I'm very personally involved with you two. That is why I don't want any garbage happening tomorrow that I'll feel hurt about. She's not as skinny as you think!' I'm telling you right now. *(Laughing)*

(Yes, Sir.)

What do you mean, "Yes, Sir?" "Yes, Sir" doesn't mean a thing. She's stout! *(Laughing)*

Wait a minute, we know the privacy, why are you laughing? You are just sitting in the Guru's presence so let me discuss it very openly. I don't want any problem at all tomorrow. And she's going to be pregnant and she's going to be this big! You understand? And you are going to be pregnant with her! I mean you are going to run around at that time because "I've got to do extra work selling stocks! And I am going to Alabama!" *(Laughing)* Do you understand what I mean?

(Yes, I do.)

Well...... I think it's okay. *(Addressing Sat Bachan Kaur.)* Any questions, dear? Don't be silent. Have you any doubt? You understand the Dharma. You understand the Khalsa woman? You understand the Grace of God? And you understand all things come from

God and all things go to God? You know the curse on this country? This country is established. You are a Canadian, so I must tell you this, this country is established on one thing, "In God we trust." You may have all the wealth, you may have all the power, but if you don't have trust in God, then you shall suffer. I repeat, You *shall* suffer. This country is based on this motto. In this land all those people who do not trust in God shall suffer. There's no way out of it. Do you understand? All your atomic energy, and Jimmy Carter,[81] and peanuts, doesn't mean anything. There's one fundamental thing in this land: "In God we trust" It is not the motto in Canada, so do you understand what I mean? And here it is most important, when you cross that border, that's it! And I'm telling you we are 250 million Americans and we *don't* trust in God; we *say* it. And if you're going to join that crowd, you're going to join those troubles too! Is that clear to you? Have you told her that? No you didn't. Why not?

HJS: I haven't had a chance, Sir. (*Laughing*)

Okay. We'll see after this chance that you do. We'll watch that. Everybody gives me permission. Does anybody have any objection to this marriage? Does anyone feel doubtful about it? Do you all honestly feel that they are mature enough and mentally fit enough to be allowed to be married? *Wahe Guru*! Well you've got a good congregation this morning. (*Laughing*) Okay let us start.

(*Traditional Wedding Shabd begins*)

The *Shabd* she has sung and she gave you this *Paala* (shawl), which is around his neck, you can see it and it is also in your hand. That means: don't let him go lousy and be a loser. That is your job! You are trusted. He trusted this man, you have the right to go over his head

and you have to fight for that right at the cost of your life. Death doesn't mean anything to us anyway. You understand? This is a commitment of yours before God! We believe that we cannot find God, but we can be found out by God, by living righteously, by living truthfully. And you have to continue to be the spirit of this man. And this *paala* has a special ceremony. You'll walk behind this man all the four rounds. That means you will not let him be stabbed and attacked and stabbed in his back! You will *guard* him! And you will see that he walks watching his front! And the day that you will forget this character you will be disloyal to your first ceremonial oath! We trust in God, we live for God, and we live within God. That is what it is. To us, the Will of God is what it is all about.

So you are marrying this man, and we are going through this ceremony. The minister has given you the *paala*, which you are holding tight in your hand. You just see that it goes around his neck and he's holding his end in his right hand. That simplifies the situation. It is better to be cautious before anything happens. You understand what I am trying to put into your head? You do not have to take it. You do not have to go along with anything which is not spiritual, which is not righteous, and you have to fight till your last breath that this man lives a truthful life. Is that clear? Is that clear to you?

You have to provide and protect her prestige at the cost of your life! No beastly action should deter you in living a precious and truthful life. You have the right to have emotions. Don't make them into commotions and then neuroses and then patterns. You have the right to make the emotions into devotions so that you can live a life of grace and ecstasy. And now today, you are holding this relationship of man and woman in the presence of God. Right? Understood? Now listen to the first law of marriage.

(First round of the Lavan is read in Gurmukhi from the Siri Guru Granth Sahib. The english translation from Peace Lagoon is read by MSS Shakti Parwha Kaur Khalsa.)

SSS Ji: Now it has begun. And it says very clearly to you that pretending to be religious and pretending that you worship God, doesn't mean a thing! You understand? It clearly says that living righteously is what God is.

Truth is great, but living in Truth is the greatest! So if you start today living as two into one consciousness, truthfully and righteously at every moment and every breath of your life, that is *all you need!* There is no need of putting ash on your head. There's no need to leave your job. There's no need for running around 'doing'...*nothing is needed!* Both of you should remember that you are creatures of God, and God is everything, and you don't need to do anything which you cannot answer for clearly in your own consciousness. Right? That's what is being said here. It is not in French, it's in English, right? What is being said in Gurmukhi is being translated to you and I'm explaining it to you simply. I'm emphasizing that you should understand that reading the Vedas, worshipping Brahma... that means worshiping for two hours, going to church, doing something, even this, coming to the Gurdwara, it's all ritualistic if every moment of your life you don't feel right, and you don't live right, and your motivation is not truth. And that is the first duty of married people, to live righteously and truth should be their guide, guardian and everything. Is that clear?

(Music starts, Couple walk around the Guru.)

SSS Ji: Nice. And you take a solemn oath that your living life shall be nothing but truth, practiced under the guidance of your very own consciousness! And you two shall merge as one in the Name of God. Almighty, Omniscient, All-prevailing. You won't shut the shutters and close the windows and think that God is not looking, that now we are in our own privacy we can do any nonsense we want. Right? Sit down. It is much better to rub you now than later. I'm just saving time, that's all.

Second Round is read.

SSS Ji: You have understood it perfectly. There is one God, within and without. Harm nobody. Be kind to everybody and defend your righteous honor at the cost of your life. You are not a slave to anybody either. You shall not bow to any man. You shall not worship any man, any statue or any situation. You shall worship only Almighty God, the Omnipresent, Omniscient One and you should feel His presence with you every minute! Period! It is a very simple thing but very difficult to do. You will not only feel the presence of God when you come to God's house, or to the church or to a synagogue or to a Gurdwara or to a temple, or to a Holy place or whatever. You shall feel the presence of God in the most filthy circumstances and the worst place. The word is *Ang Sung Wahe Guru*, "Within every limb and every fiber of my body, God lives."

Singing begins and the second round is walked. The couple bows and is seated. The Third round is read from the Guru. The English translation is read.

SSS Ji: The third round is in the simplest English. You must have the entire wealth of the world, but don't claim it! Keep it as a trustee, in the Name of God. Because if you'll be earthbound then you'll be earth bound and then you'll never be in a position to go any other bound. And you have to ultimately understand that you have to merge with the Boundless—that is God. I'm saying to you that you live in tattered clothes and look poor and be a beggar and you think you are great; you are a nuisance! I'm asking you to realize the entire potential of your life. Earn enough, and share with those who are unfortunate—who are not in a position to do it—so that you can inspire them from your example to do that! I'm asking you...you can have all the wealth of the world, but remember this shall not go with you. Do you understand? Therefore your home should be a home of grace, divinity and dignity, morals and character, and it must represent to somebody who is very innocent and unknowingly knows you and wants to know you, that he is entering premises where God rules: That's a very simple example! You understand that? Fine.

Music begins and the third round is taken around the Guru.

SSS Ji: You are doing this marriage ceremony in the name of God—by the Will of God and by the virtues of God. So God is your beginning, your now, and your ultimate. Because that is what the purpose of life is. We do not have to compete with the lustful living in our land. We have to compete to inherit in our mind and heart, the first motto, "In God we trust and in God we live." We all came here for one purpose, to worship God freely, and that is what we intend to do. That is what both of you have to do. Have faith that God has not abandoned you. You are not to do weird things to look holy. You simply have to control your nine holes and administer them as the master of your mind and see that what comes in is pure and what goes out has to go. That is the rational, logical and reasonable way to live as human beings. You'll read now.

Fourth round read, music played, and fourth walk taken.

By the power conferred on me by the holiest of the holy—The Holy Akal Takhat—and so recognized by the superior Supreme Court of Washington, D.C. and also in the State of California, as a minister of Sikh religion and having tested you and having questioned you and having had you go through all of this ceremony required by the religion…and in the presence of the Holy Siri Guru Granth I find you to have gone through this ceremony according to my satisfaction, I find you now as husband and wife. It is my prayer that you may live in that unity which you have promised to do as man and woman. It will be recorded in all the records of this County and State and you'll be honored as a man and wife. That's your promise in the court of God. Bless you, and may you live long and have peace.

   Sat Nam.

CHAPTER FIFTEEN

ABOUT YOGI BHAJAN

YOGI BHAJAN, TEACHER OF TEACHERS
Yogi Bhajan touched the hearts and opened the minds of people in all walks of life. Equally at home in a Board Room or teaching in a park sitting on the grass, he was mentor to statesmen, politicians and CEO's, confidante of religious leaders, media personalities, and simple seekers. His motto was, "It's not the life that matters, it's the courage that you bring to it," the opening lines from a book he read when he was nine years old.[82] His bottom line, printed on the back of his calling card: "If you can't see God in all, you can't see God at all." And he lived it.

Yogi Bhajan was born Harbhajan Singh Puri in India on August 26, 1929. During early childhood he learned at the knee of his saintly grandfather. When he was eight he was sent to study with the great Master, Sant Hazara Singh, under whose unrelenting tutelage the boy mastered Kundalini Yoga at 16-1/2.

During the partition of India in 1947, young Harbhajan's village had to be evacuated because it was to become a part of Pakistan. Still a teenager, his leadership ability was already recognized, and he was put in charge of bringing more than a thousand people to safety in Delhi, traveling through many dangerous miles of a country in violent upheaval.

At Punjab University he won prizes in debate (of course), was a champion athlete, and earned his Masters degree in Economics. In the Indian Army he was a Motor Transport Officer and then served the Indian Government in the Tax and Customs division until he came to the West. He married Bibi Inderjit Kaur in 1953. They had three children born in India and five grandchildren born in the United States.

At his first public lecture in the United States on January 5, 1969, Yogi Bhajan proclaimed, "It is your birthright to be healthy, happy, and holy; Kundalini Yoga is the way to claim it."

It was the dawning of the Aquarian Age. Seeing what the future was going to bring, he was determined to train leaders and teachers with the power to heal, uplift, and inspire humanity. He said, "I've come to train teachers, not to get disciples." He taught Kundalini Yoga openly to the public for the first time in history, despite the taboo that had kept it shrouded in secrecy for centuries.

He didn't just teach physical exercises, meditation, and yogic breathing techniques as such, he taught people how to live, how to relate to each other, and how to relate to God. The 3HO way of life offered an alternative to the prevalent drug culture. In July of 1969 he legally established the "3HO" Foundation, an acronym for the Healthy, Happy, Holy Organization.

Yogi Bhajan championed the cause of World Peace, worked to unite spiritual leaders of all faiths, and insisted upon restoring women to their rightful place of dignity and respect in society. He started a summer camp for women in order, as he said, to "change Chicks into Eagles." He inspired women to lead, uplift, and heal through their inherent grace and power. In 1970, he created the Grace of God Movement for the Women of America (GGMWA) with its own body of teachings especially for women.

His penetrating insight, infinite compassion, tireless service, and delightful sense of humor immediately endeared him to the eager young people who flocked to his Kundalini Yoga classes. His fiery determination to awaken their souls and teach them never to settle for less than the best within themselves had a powerful impact. He taught students how to access their intuitive awareness, how to experience higher consciousness without drugs, and how to build a future for themselves and their families. He told them, "Be ten times greater than me." He also said, "Don't love me; love my teachings."

In 1973 he founded 3HO SuperHealth, the only holistic substance abuse treatment program of its kind. It was accredited by the U.S. Joint Commission on Accreditation of Healthcare Organizations.

During this lifetime, Yogi Bhajan went from riches to rags and back again. As a real Yogi, not affected by the pairs of opposites, he lived in his own majesty throughout all the tests and trials that confronted him, affirming with absolute conviction that every-thing is God's will.

He never took credit for any of his achievements; always saying it was all the grace of God and Guru, that he was "just the mailman delivering the message."

Yogi Bhajan not only trained thousands of Kundalini Yoga Teachers throughout the

world, but also created an entire sub-culture within the mainstream population, a 3HO "family" committed to living consciously and righteously.

Poet, philosopher, seer, sage, saint, healer, religious leader, counselor, artist, author, lecturer, and even an excellent cook, Yogi Bhajan was, first and foremost, always a Teacher with a capital T.

He published over 30 books and over 200 other books, videos, and CDs feature his teachings. Known as the "Father of the Woodstock nation," in 1980 he earned his Ph.D. in the Psychology of Communication.

He was definitely not the stereotype of a yogi from a cave, wearing a loincloth and carrying a begging bowl. On the contrary, he inspired and was the driving force behind 19 thriving corporations all of which espouse the principles he taught. These conscious businesses offer services including computer systems, security, and counseling, plus a mail order catalog presenting a wide array of health food and other products, including the Peace Cereals, Yogi Teas, herbal remedies, and massage oils, based on formulas Yogi Bhajan developed.

After becoming the only living Mahan Tantric (Master of White Tantric Yoga™) in 1971, he traveled to different cities 50 weekends out of every year to conduct White Tantric Yoga™ courses. Practically living in airplanes took its toll, and by 1987 he needed triple by-pass heart surgery. As soon as he recovered, he began putting the dynamic White Tantric Yoga™ meditations on videotape, sending representatives all over the world to facilitate his workshops. He was, and still is, the only Master empowered to teach White Tantric Yoga™, which he does through his subtle body. The transformational impact of the tantric energy on the participants today is perhaps even stronger now that he is no longer limited by his physical body.

Although he himself was a devoted Sikh, Yogi Bhajan never tried to convert anyone. It is against the tenets of the Sikh religion to proselytize. However, his example of unshakable faith and commitment to his God and Guru was contagious, and many of his students recognized they were destined to walk through life on the Sikh path.

In 1971, at Amritsar, India, a prominent Sikh leader honored him by giving him the first ever title of "Siri Singh Sahib." He returned to the U.S. as the Chief Religious and Administrative Authority for Sikh Dharma of the Western Hemisphere, and took on the responsibility of establishing a Sikh Ministry in the West.

Promoting world peace, he met with religious and spiritual leaders all over the world. He served in the World Parliament of Religions and was co-president and host of Human Unity Conferences. In 1983 he founded International Peace Prayer Day, an annual interfaith celebration that now draws over a thousand people to Ram Das Puri, sacred land nestled in the Jemez Mountains of New Mexico. He was awarded the Massachusetts Peace Abbey Courage of Conscience Award in 1995.

In 1979, honoring his 50th Birthday, a volume titled *The Man Called the Siri Singh Sahib* detailed the outstanding achievements of Yogi Bhajan's first ten years as a Teacher in the West. There is yet to be written a full account of this amazing man's service to humanity.

This attempt to tell about Yogi Bhajan would not be complete without emphasizing his delightful sense of humor. He was charming and funny, and often had everyone in gales of laughter. He believed in having fun and made any occasion into a party. Going with him shopping, to a restaurant or to the movies was always an adventure, usually involving at least a dozen people and a caravan of vehicles all trying to keep up with him.

Yogi Bhajan left his body on October 6, 2004, at the age of 75. To be honest, I can't say he "died," because his presence is still so vibrantly with us. His divine wisdom and inspiration live on in the enlightened legacy of the vast library of teachings he created to serve us now, and for countless generations to come.

JOINT RESOLUTION OF CONGRESS HONORS YOGI BHAJAN

In the history of the United States Congress, only a handful of spiritual leaders have ever merited a Joint Resolution honoring their life and work. They include Martin Luther King, Pope John Paul II, and Mother Teresa. Siri Singh Sahib, Bhai Sahib Harbhajan Singh Khalsa Yogiji, known as Yogi Bhajan, has now joined the ranks of those who have received such an honor.

News Release
U.S. SENATORS JEFF BINGAMAN AND PETE DOMENICI

FOR IMMEDIATE RELEASE: Thursday, April 7, 2005
SENATE APPROVES RESOLUTION TO HONOR YOGI BHAJAN

WASHINGTON – The U.S. Senate has approved a Congressional resolution introduced by U.S. Senators Jeff Bingaman and Pete Domenici that honors the late Sikh leader Yogi Bhajan. Rep. Tom Udall introduced the same resolution in the House of Representatives. That measure passed the House on Tuesday.

"Yogi Bhajan was the beloved spiritual leader of thousands of Western Sikhs," Bingaman said. "This Congressional resolution recognizes his distinguished life and the importance of his teachings."

"This is a lasting tribute to an influential spiritual leader who contributed greatly to the promotion of peace. Yogi Bhajan was an inspirational figure and a proud legacy for New Mexicans who remember his hopeful message and practice his teachings of humanity," Domenici said.

One Hundred Ninth Congress
of the
United States of America
AT THE FIRST SESSION

Begun and held at the City of Washington on Tuesday, the fourth day of January, two thousand and five

Concurrent Resolution
Resolved by the House of Representatives (the Senate concurring) that the Congress

Recognizes that the teachings of Yogi Bhajan about Sikhism and yoga, and the businesses formed under his inspiration, improved the personal, political, spiritual, and professional relations between citizens of the United States and the citizens of India;

Recognizes the legendary compassion, wisdom, kindness, and courage of Yogi Bhajan, and his wealth of accomplishments on behalf of the Sikh community; and

Extends its condolences to Inderjit Kaur, the wife of Yogi Bhajan, his 3 children and 5 grandchildren, and to Sikh and "Healthy, Happy, Holy Organization (3HO)" communities around the Nation and the world upon the death on October 6, 2004, of Yogi Bhajan, an individual who was a wise teacher and mentor, an outstanding pioneer, a champion of peace, and a compassionate human being.

H.Con.Res.34   Agreed to April 6, 2005

To view the Resolution in its entirety, log on to www.sikhner.com/yogibhajan

YOGI BHAJAN MEMORIAL HIGHWAY

As you head north from Santa Fe, New Mexico, on Highway 84 toward Espanola, where the DreamCatcher Theater sits at the top of the hill at the turn-off to reach Hacienda de Guru Ram Das, you will see a sign saying YOGI BHAJAN MEMORIAL HIGHWAY. In August of 2005, as we celebrated what would have been Yogi Bhajan's 76th birthday, it was announced that Highway 106, which borders Hacienda de Guru Ram Das, Yogi Bhajan's home in Espanola, has been renamed the YOGI BHAJAN MEMORIAL HIGHWAY by the Governor of New Mexico, Bill Richardson.

APPENDIX

GUIDE TO PRONUNCIATION

A   = rhymes with the "u" in up

AA   = sounds like the "a" in "father"

I   = short sound like the "i" in "is"

U   = is like the "u" in "put" or "push"

O   = rhymes with "oat" or "coat"

OO   = sounds like the "oo" in "ooze"

AI   = kind of like "at" or "apple" (not like "ay" in hay)

E or AY   = both are pronounced "ay" to rhyme with "hay" – the thing horses eat! (Both E and AY are used in various transliterations, and are both pronounced to rhyme with "say")

SAT NAM spelled phonetically would be Sat Naam

GLOSSARY

3HO: the Healthy, Happy, Holy Organization, a non-profit corporation dedicated to serving humanity through the teachings of Kundalini Yoga and the 3HO lifestyle as taught by Yogi Bhajan

Ajna: see Brow Point

Akal: deathless

Akashic Records: etheric records where all actions and thoughts are recorded

Ambrosial Hours: the 2-1/2 hours before sunrise

Amrit: nectar of bliss (Amrit is given in the ceremony in which Sikhs pledge to live as Khalsa)

Anand: soulful bliss

Apana: the outgoing or eliminating breath

Aquarian Age: Age of "I know. I want to experience." (Follows the Piscean Age)

Arcline: the 6th energy body extends from one earlobe across the hairline and brow to the other earlobe and represents the projecting power of the mind, intuition, and the power of prayer. Women have a second Arcline from breast to breast.

Asana: yogic posture; way of sitting

Ashram: literally, "the house of the teacher" providing a spiritual community that supports mind/body/spirit health and growth

Ashtang Mantra: (Ashtang means "eight") Sound current with eight syllables. See EK ONG KAR SAT NAM SIRI WAHE GURU

Aura: the energy field that surrounds and interpenetrates the body, also called the electro-magnetic field

Ayurveda: a holistic system of medicine, from the Sanskrit words meaning "life" and "knowledge," or the knowledge of life

Bandh: lock or knot

Bhakti Yoga: yogic path of Devotion

Bij Mantra: seed sound, such as "Sat Nam"

Breath of Fire: a pranayam consisting of continuous rapid nostril breathing, two to three breaths per second, while pulling the navel point in on the exhale and relaxing it on the inhale; it is used to energize the nervous system and purify the bloodstream

Brow Point: also called the Ajna, or the Third Eye, located at the root of the nose, between the eyebrows, and up about 1/8 inch

Chakras: eight energy centers located at: 1) base of the spine between the rectum and sex organs, 2) sex organs, 3) navel point, 4) center of the chest between the nipples, 5) throat, 6) brow point, 7) crown (top) of the head, 8) electromagnetic field surrounding the body

Cosmos: harmonious systematic universe

Crown Chakra: the seventh chakra at the top of the head

Darshan: blessing of seeing or being seen by a Holy personage

Deep Relaxation: as important as exercise or meditation, deep relaxation helps release stress from both the mind and the body, adjusts the glandular balance, and allows the body's natural self-healing energy to function, resulting in mental clarity and physical ease

Dharma: spiritual path, righteousness, justice, harmony, eternal truth.

Diaphragm Lock: see Uddiyana Bandh

Easy Pose: a comfortable cross-legged sitting position; *Sukhasan*

EK ONG KAR SAT NAM SIRI WHA GURU was the original pronunciation Yogi Bhajan taught. However, he later taught everyone to pronounce it as *"Wha-hay Guroo"* in conformity with the way it is written in the Gurmukhi script (adding the short "hay" vowel). He also then taught it to be done in 2-1/2 breaths. Also see *Ashtang Mantra*.

Electromagnetic Field: energy field that surrounds the body in the same way the Earth's magnetic field envelops the Earth. The electromagnetic field is also called the Aura, and when it is strong, it attracts positive energy, and protects from negativity and illness.

God: Generator, Organizer, and Destroyer or Deliverer of all Creation

Golden Temple: most revered and sacred Sikh temple in the world (*Hari Mandir Sahib*) in Amritsar India

Gunas: the three fundamental attributes or qualities that permeate and infuse all life: *Sattva* (essence), *Rajas* (activity), *Tamas* (inertia)

Gurbani: sacred language based on the power of the sound current

Gurdwara: Sikh temple or place of worship, the "gate of the Guru"

Gurmukhi: sacred script (alphabet) based on the transformative power of the sound current; literally, "from the mouth of the Guru"

Guru: Gu means darkness; Ru means light: i.e., the dispeller of ignorance; Teacher: the giver of technology

Guru Nanak: the first of the ten Sikh Gurus, a saint, poet, and minstrel, and Teacher of the Sikh lifestyle

Guru Ram Das: the 4th Sikh Guru, the embodiment of compassion, humility, integrity and service, known for his healing power as "The Lord of Miracles"

Gyan Mudra: mudra that is said to activate the wisdom and knowledge areas of the brain; the tip of the thumb touches the index finger and the rest of the fingers are straight

Gyan Yoga: yogic path of the intellect

Har: one of the names of God in His creative aspect; (Har does not rhyme with car, but rather the "a" is short like the "u" in rug, and the "r" is created by flicking the tongue to the roof of the mouth like a rolled "r" in Spanish)

Hatha Yoga: yogic path primarily utilizing physical postures

Heart Center: 4th Chakra

Jaap Sahib: epic prayer/poem written in praise of God by Guru Gobind Singh, 10th Sikh Guru

Jalandhar Bandh: Neck Lock; stretch the back of the neck gently straight by pulling the chin straight back and lifting the chest

Jap: repeat or recite

Japji (Japji Sahib): "song of the soul"; one of five Sikh prayers recited daily to connect with one's own soul; composed by Guru Nanak

Jetha: a group of travelers on a spiritual journey, usually musicians

Kali Yug: the current period of the world time cycle lasting 432,000 years, the Age of conflict

Karma: the cosmic law of cause and effect, action and reaction

Khalsa: pure ones (Brotherhood established by Guru Gobind Singh in 1699)

Khalsa Women's Training Camp: (KWTC, Khalsa Women's Training Camp) spiritual camp for women held annually in New Mexico by 3HO, plus at other locations throughout the world, such as Mexico and Canada

Kirtan: sacred music

KRI: Kundalini Research Institute, the non-profit organization dedicated to the preservation of the teachings of Yogi Bhajan

Kriya: literally, "completed action"; combination of yogic posture, hand position, mantra, breathing, and rhythm; designed to bring about a specific effect on the body, mind, and consciousness; a *kriya* may be one specific exercise or a designated sequence of exercises

Kundalini: the energy that lies at the base of the spine, the creative consciousness experienced when the energies of the glandular and nervous systems combine to create total awareness, the energy of the soul; literally means "the curl in the lock of the hair of the beloved"

Laya Yoga: a form of meditation using rhythmic mantra patterns and bandhs (locks)

Liberation: the experience of your own Infinity

Long Deep Breathing: long deep slow rhythmic breath; the abdomen expands at the start of the inhale and contracts at the end of the exhale

Mahan Tantric: Master of White Tantric Yoga (such as Yogi Bhajan), the only person qualified to conduct White Tantric Yoga Courses (he now teaches on video, through his subtle body); there can only be one living Mahan Tantric at any given time

Mala: string of beads used as a meditation tool

Mantra: a syllable or combination of syllables that help focus the mind; mantras can be audible or silent

Maya: the illusion that we mistake for reality; literally "anything measurable"

Meditation: the process of controlling and transcending the thoughts, which leads to increased focus, mental relaxation, and clarity; letting God talk to you

Miri Piri: temporal/spiritual balance of the Universe

Moon Centers: physical areas or points located on the human body, sensitive to lunar energies. (Men have only one, located at the chin. Women have eleven, which affect their emotional state)

Morning Call: another name for the Ashtang Mantra, the 2-1/2 cycle breath "long" *Ek Ong Kar* chant

Mudra: Yogic hand position

Mulbandh: Root Lock, used to close off the lower three chakras allowing the kundalini energy to flow upwards; (simultaneously contract the muscles of the rectum, sex organs, lower abdomen, and navel point

Mul Mantra: First lines of *Japji Sahib*

Naad: basic sound for all languages, originating from the sound current; the secrets hidden in sound

Nadhis: subtle nerve channels

Neck Lock: see *Jalandhar Bandh*

Neutral Mind: the mind that judges and assesses without attachment in relation to either fear or wishful thinking; it observes the actions of both the negative and positive minds, and then makes decisions in relationship to the higher self

Parkarma: walkway surrounding the Golden Temple in Amritsar, India

Patanjali: first yogi to record the eight limbs of Raja Yoga, the Yoga Sutras of Patanjali written in the second Century B.C. (The book *How to Know God* is based on Patanjali's yoga sutras)

Pauri: steps of knowledge guiding one to experience God consciousness

Piscean Age: Age of "I want to know. I need to learn."

Prana: the life force or vital air above the navel center

Pooja: ritual worship

Pranayam: yogic breathing technique, such as Long Deep Breathing or Breath of Fire

Prasad (Prashad): sacred gift

Prayer: talking to God

Raga: traditional Indian spiritual music in a tonal system in which variations are improvised within a prescribed framework of progressions, melodic formulas, and rhythmic patterns

Ragi: one who plays sacred Indian music

Raj Yoga: royal path of Yoga; mental path

Rishi: a sage or saint in India

Rock Pose: Yogic posture sitting on your heels; *Vajrasan*

Root Lock: see *Mulbandh*

Sadhana: regular daily spiritual practice

Sangat: community of like-minded people; group or gathering

Sat Nam: true identity

Sat Nam Rasayan: healing art based on the application of the meditative transcendent mind; from Sanskrit, meaning "universal remedy of manifested truth"

Sattva: one of the three gunas or qualities, meaning pure, calm, and clear

Saturn Teacher: shows the student the path to his or her destiny without compromise

Sensory Human: the fully-functioning human, intuitively aware, self-validated, and authentic

Seva: selfless service

Shabd: sound current, Divine word/s

Shabd Guru: sacred volume of writings; source of spiritual wisdom and guidance (Siri Guru Granth Sahib)

Shakti: woman; feminine aspect of God; God's power in manifestation

Sikh: literally a seeker of Truth

Sikh Dharma: youngest of the major world religions, founded by Guru Nanak; based on the belief in One God, conscious living, equality of mankind, and respect for all religions

Siri Guru Granth Sahib: revered as the living Guru for Sikhs, this volume contains sacred words spoken by enlightened beings while in a state of Divine Union (yoga) with God.

Summer Solstice Sadhana: annual 3HO Kundalini Yoga camp held in New Mexico at the time of the summer solstice.

Sutra: selection from sacred writings; literally "thread"

Tattwas: qualities associated with earth, water, fire, air, and ether

Third Eye: see Brow Point

Tuning in: each Kundalini Yoga session begins with at least three repetitions of the Adi Mantra: *Ong Namo Guru Dev Namo*, an invocation calling upon the Creator and the Divine Teacher within

Uddiyana Bandh: Diaphragm Lock, applied on the exhale by lifting the chest and pulling the diaphragm muscle (the area above the navel) up and in

Upanishads: writings which form the last section of the literature of the Vedas, composed beginning 900 B.C.; the basis for the later philosophical schools of Vedanta

Vedanta: one of the six classical systems of Indian philosophy

Vedas: ancient Hindu scriptures

Venus Kriyas: special advanced exercises taught by Yogi Bhajan, done with a partner

Venus Lock: mudra (hand position) with fingers interlaced; for men, the left thumb is on the webbing between the right thumb and the index finger while the right thumb is on the fleshy mound of the left hand just below where the (left) thumb begins. Reverse for women.

Wahe Guru: mantra of ecstasy expressing the inexpressible magnificence of God ("Wow! God is great beyond description!")

White Tantric Yoga: meditation workshop for healing and transmuting subconscious thought patterns and expanding awareness, taught only by the Mahan Tantric.

Women's Camp: (KWTC, Khalsa Women's Training Camp) spiritual camp for women held annually in New Mexico by 3HO, plus at other locations throughout the world, such as Mexico and Canada

Yatra: spiritual journey; pilgrimage

Yoga: union: the science of yoking or uniting the individual consciousness with the Universal consciousness

Yogi Tea: healing formula beverage made from cinnamon, cardamom, black peppercorns, cloves (ginger root is optional), and milk; the original recipe also calls for black tea

Yogini: female practitioner of yoga

Yug (Yuga): Sanskrit term for an "Age" meaning one of the four periods into which the world time cycle is divided: Sat Yug, Treta Yug, Doapar Yug, Kali Yug

CHAPTER NOTES

INTRODUCTION
[1] Male/Female principles; the entire quote is from the contemporaneous notes of Guru Rattan Kaur Khalsa, and could not be verified by KRI review.

[2] Yogi Bhajan. At KWTC he called this the "Greatest Thing of the Day" (GTD) and the women at camp wrote a song, "One Thing to Remember is: All Things Come from God..."

CHAPTER 2   LEARNING TO BE HUMAN
[3] Traditional quote from yogic scriptures

[4] This was where I got the sub-title for this book!

CHAPTER 3   UNION
[5] The Aquarian Teacher; page 235

[6] Sexuality and Spirituality by Dr. Gururattan Kaur Khalsa and Ann Marie Maxwell

CHAPTER 4   RECIPE FOR HAPPINESS
[7] Translated by Yogi Bhajan from words of Guru Arjan Dev in Siri Guru Granth Sahib

[8] See Chapter 8: "Yogic Technology to the Rescue"

[9] Defined by Yogi Bhajan; Reprinted from *Kundalini Yoga: The Flow of Eternal Power* by Shakti Parwha Kaur Khalsa

[10] For additional topics (and some the same) see page 68

[11] Man to Man Part 4 "Growing as a Man" page 26

[12] Man to Man Part 4 "Growing as a Man" page 31

[13] Be honest, of course, but no need to go into intimate details if you've had previous relationships.

CHAPTER 5   WORDS FOR WOMEN
[14] Available from Ancient Healing Ways – see "Sources and Resources"

[15] Shakti: Feminine aspect of God; God's power in manifestation; every woman is a "shakti"

[16] See GGM meditation; Chapter 9: Yogic Technology to the Rescue

[17] Aquarian Teacher Page 235

[18] From Man to Man P. 17, part 2, "Inside the Real Man"

[19] Arcline: see Glossary

[20] See page 93 in Chapter 11 "Yogic Technology to the Rescue"

[21] Chapter 12: "Up Close and Personal"

[22] Dates of Yogi Bhajan's lectures from which quotes were taken:
7/4/79; 7/5/79; 7/18/79; 7/21/76; 8/4/75; 8/13/78

CHAPTER 6   MESSAGES FOR MEN

23 Man to Man Part 2 "Inside the Real Man".

24 Man to Man: 1978-1984

25 Man to Man Part 2, page 8

26 See "Methods for Men" page 106

27 Arcline: See Glossary

28 See page 106, Methods for Men" (from pages 120,121 *Kundalini Postures and Poetry*)

29 Page 58 Man to Man Part 4:

30 Man to Man Part 4 P.34

31 According to ancient tradition, the soul enters the mother's womb on the 120th day of pregnancy. In 3HO we hold 120th day celebrations. It's not a baby shower. Gifts are brought for the mother to be, honoring her personally and cosmically for her sacred role. Prayers are offered that she may bring a saint, a hero, or a giver into the world!

32 Man to Man Part 4, page 65

33 Man to Man, page 18

34 Man to Man Part 2, page 12

35 Moon Centers: *See Glossary*

36 Historically, it is indicated that Kipling wrote "If" as a tribute to the qualities of Dr. Leander Starr Jamison

CHAPTER 7   CHALLENGES IN MARRIAGE

37 Though Yogi Bhajan strongly recommends having the woman handle the finances.

38 Amrit: Sikh vows to live as Khalsa; analogous to "baptism," but voluntarily chosen by the individual (ceremony not given automatically at birth)

39 Yogi Bhajan: Women in Training, "Crossing the Crossroads of Crisis" 1987, page 109

40   Page 61 Chapter 9: Professionally Speaking

CHAPTER 8   SEX AND SEXUALITY

41 From Yogi Bhajan's Lecture: "There's Nothing in Sex and Without Sex There is Nothing," page 52

42 Ancient yogic wisdom teaches that eating garlic increases the production of semen in the body

43 See page 100, Yogic Technology to the Rescue

44 See page 101, Yogic Technology to the Rescue

CHAPTER 9   PROFESSIONALLY SPEAKING

45 Sardarni Sahiba: Sikh Ministerial title

46 Kundalini Research Institute

47 (MFT = Marriage and Family Therapist)

48 Earth, Water, Fire, Air, Ether: Five Elements in every human being and they correspond to five of our energy centers (Chakras).

49 See page 102

50 See Glossary

CHAPTER 10   WHEN YOGI BHAJAN SPEAKS

51 Wedding taking place in a Gurdwara, with Siri Guru Granth Sahib *(see Glossary)* presiding

52 This is typical of Yogi Bhajan – to seemingly contradict something he has said elsewhere; i.e., he has often referred to marriage as a "merger!"

53 Methods by which Sikhs were martyred

54 Sikh Wedding Ceremony: see page 134

55 Sikh Wedding Ceremony: see page 134

56 Guru Amar Das, Siri Guru Granth Sahib, page 788.

CHAPTER 11   THINGS TO DO

57 Reprinted from "Kundalini Rising"

58 Recorded version available from Ancient Healing Ways *(See Sources and Resources)*

59 Raag is a prescribed traditional musical form

60 See Appendix for pronunciation guide

61 Locks: see Mulbandh, Jalandhar Bandh in Glossary

62 Aquarian Teacher; page 97

63 Prana, Pranee, Pranayam; page 192

64 Available on CD. *(See Sources and Resources)*

CHAPTER 12   UP CLOSE AND PERSONAL: REAL STORIES

65 Traditional Sikh affirmation: "Khalsa belongs to God; Victory belongs to God"

66 See page 104

67 *Bana*: Clothing that identifies the wearer as a Sikh

68 See page 93

69 Peace Lagoon: English translation of traditional Sikh prayers; Lavan: Wedding vows *(see page 135)*

70 Sacred Music

71 Siri Guru Granth Sahib

72 Individual Soul

73 Universal Soul

74 Kundalini Yoga: The Flow of Eternal Power by Shakti P.K. Khalsa; Ashtang Mantra: see Glossary

75 Ministerial title. (Commemorative Volume, *The Man Called The Siri Singh Sahib,* was published in 1979)

76 Karma: Law of Cause and Effect; results of choices made: "As you sow, so shall you reap"

77 I kept up with *Science of Keeping Up* for 30 years

78 The latter is waiting for a Publisher!

CHAPTER 13   THE WEDDING

79 Sanskrit name for God in His Creative Aspect

80 Next: You can read what Yogi Bhajan said when he conducted Sat Bachan Kaur's wedding to Hari Jiwan Singh! Wow! page 142

CHAPTER 14   YOGI BHAJAN CONDUCTS A WEDDING

81 Then President of the United States

CHAPTER 15   ABOUT YOGI BHAJAN

82 *Fortitude* by Hugh Walpole

SOURCES & RESOURCES

BOOKS • VIDEOS • CD'S • TRANSCRIPTS

ANCIENT HEALING WAYS
CD's Music and Mantras
Kundalini Yoga Books, CD's and Videos
Yogi Bhajan's Video Lectures and Transcripts
KWTC transcripts; "Grace of God Manual"
www.a-healing.com
1-800-359-2940

SPIRIT VOYAGE MUSIC
Music for Yoga, Meditation, and Joy
Celebrate Peace Concerts and Workshops
with Snatam and Guru Ganesha
Concert Tickets, Schedules, Information & CD's
www.SpiritVoyage.com

EVENTS

3HO FOUNDATION
Calendar of Events, lifestyle,
Kundalini Yoga, Yogi Bhajan
Links to KWTC, IKYTA, KRI
www.3ho.org

INTERNATIONAL PEACE PRAYER DAY
Information, Photo gallery, Grant recipients
www.peacecereal.com

SUGGESTED READING

SACRED SEXUAL BLISS

By Dr. Sat-Kaur Khalsa

Marriage, family, and child psychotherapist, Dr. Sat-Kaur, combines insights from her professional psychological training with deep spiritual awareness. She studied directly under guidance of Yogi Bhajan for over 34 years.

Published by Yogi Ji Press, PO Box 970, Santa Cruz, NM 87567 ISBN # 0-9655523-2-2

AQUARIAN TIMES MAGAZINE

featuring Prosperity Paths, Kundalini Yoga, Health, Inspiration, Meditations

Free Subscription

www.AT-PP@kiit.com

P.O. Box 385   Santa Cruz, NM 87567

THE AQUARIAN TEACHER

This two volume work is virtually an encyclopedia – a marvelous and accessible source of information, clarification, and explanation of Kundalini Yoga as taught by Yogi Bhajan.® Used in KRI International Kundalini Yoga Teacher Training, one volume is the "Textbook," the other, the "Yoga Manual." Chock full of mantras and meditations for specifics.

Published by KRI   ISBN 0-9720110-1-3

THE TEACHINGS OF YOGI BHAJAN

"A Practical demonstration of the power of the spoken Word."

An inspiring and powerful collection of Yogi Bhajan's quotable quotes. He said, "This book has been written with one intention, to take people from a negative state of mind to a positive one."

Published by Arcline   ISBN 0-895090-52-X

KUNDALINI YOGA: THE FLOW OF ETERNAL POWER

By Shakti Parwha Kaur Khalsa

This is an easy, simple introduction and guide to the "Yoga of Awareness." Reader friendly!

A Perigee Book Published by the Berkley Publishing Group ISBN 0-399-52420-7

SOME OTHER VIEWS!

Yogi Bhajan used to say, "Life is a comparative study." The following books about marriage don't mention meditation, mantra, or yoga, but I found them fascinating reading, and their experiences worth sharing. I was particularly intrigued by these four:

I MARRIED MY MOTHER-IN-LAW
AND OTHER TALES OF IN-LAWS WE CAN'T LIVE WITH – AND CAN'T LIVE WITHOUT
Edited by Ilena Silverman
The title tells it all! The authors are all professional writers; their essays are in-depth and quite revealing.
Published by Riverhead books/ Penguin Group   ISBN 1-59448-909-2

THE PROPER CARE AND FEEDING OF HUSBANDS
by Dr. Laura Schlessinger
This book, a #1 National Best Seller, has sold over a million copies. (Now that I've read it, I know why!) Dr. Laura emphasizes the difference between men and women, and the power women have to create and maintain a happy marriage. She provides "real life examples and real life solutions." I often listen to the practical and valuable advice she gives to callers on her radio show in Los Angeles. (She doesn't pull any punches.)

THE PROPER CARE AND FEEDING OF MARRIAGE
by Dr. Laura Schlessinger
This book reinforces and elaborates by numerous examples many of the basic principles of human behavior that Yogi Bhajan taught: emphasizing the effectiveness of practicing such values as kindness, consideration, and the greatest happiness coming from giving to your spouse.

SPOUSE: THE TRUTH ABOUT MARRIAGE
by Shobhaa De
The author, a well known Indian writer, provides an intimate look at modern Indian (Hindu) married life from her perspective as a happily married wife and mother plus successful career woman.
First Published by Penguin books in India – 2005

* * *

SHAKTI PARWHA KAUR KHALSA
sparwha@sbcglobal.net